Printed in Dallas, Texas by The Odee Company

Contact: contact@first15.org
www.first15.org

Layout Designed by Matt Ravenelle
mattravenelle.com

Images curated from
Unsplash

ABOUT FIRST15

Spending time alone with God every day can be a struggle. We're busier – and more stressed – than ever. But still, we know it's important to spend time alone with our Creator. We know we need to read his word, pray, and worship him.

First15 bridges the gap between desire and reality, helping you establish the rhythm of meaningful, daily experiences in God's presence. First15 answers the critical questions:

• Why should I spend time alone with God?
• How do I spend time alone with God?
• How do I get the most out of my time alone with God?
• How can I become more consistent with my time alone with God?

And by answering these questions through the format of daily devotionals, you'll practice the rhythm of meeting with God while experiencing the incredible gift of his loving presence given to those who make time to meet with him.

Allow God's passionate pursuit to draw you in across the next several days. And watch as every day is better than the last as your life is built on the solid foundation of God's love through the power of consistent, meaningful time alone with him.

To learn more about First15, visit our website first15. org. First15 is available across mobile app, email, podcast, and our website. Subscribe to our devotional today and experience God in a fresh way every day.

―――――――――――

ABOUT THE AUTHOR

Craig Denison is the author of First15, a daily devotional guiding over a million believers into a fresh experience with God every day. In 2015, Craig founded First15 after sensing a longing in God's heart for his people to be about relationship – real, restored relationship with him – that above all else, he simply wanted the hearts of his people. Craig began praying, dreaming, and writing. And the idea of helping people spend the first fifteen minutes of their day focusing on nothing else but growing in their relationship with God was born. The vision was birthed in Craig's heart that if we as a people would worship, read, and pray at the beginning of every day, everything could change for the better. Craig writes, speaks, and he and his wife, Rachel lead worship to help believers establish a more tangible, meaningful connection with God.

———————

CONTENTS

Jesus' High Priestly prayer

"He is able to save to the uttermost those
who draw near to God through him, since he
always lives to make intercession for them."
Hebrews 7:25

WEEKLY OVERVIEW

We have a great High Priest who constantly intercedes on our behalf. The Son of God and Man loves you more deeply than you can fathom. He prays for you, that you might walk in the abundant life his death affords you. And in John 17 we get a glimpse into the fullness of his desire for all those who would believe in him. As we dive deeply into the riches of Jesus' High Priestly prayer this week, may your heart be awakened and your life be transformed by the riches of God's love.

The Authority of King Jesus

DAY 1

DEVOTIONAL

John 17:1-2 marks the beginning of one of the most powerful passages in all of Scripture. Jesus prays to the Father and says, *"Father, the hour has come: glorify your Son that the Son may glorify you, since you have given him authority over all flesh, to give eternal life to all whom you have given him."* Jesus knows that his time on the earth is coming to a close. He knows that he must sacrifice his life so that the door to restored relationship with the Father would be flung open to all who would put their faith in him.

"When Jesus had spoken these words, he lifted up his eyes to heaven, and said, 'Father, the hour has come; glorify your Son that the Son may glorify you, since you have given him authority over all flesh, to give eternal life to all whom you have given him.'"

JOHN 17:1-2

What good news it is that the Father has given the Son *"authority over all flesh."* You and I serve the one true King of all mankind. Jesus is King of all the earth. And our King is one who would ask the Father to send him to die that we might live. Our King willfully lays down his life for us who have done nothing to deserve his kindness. Colossians 1:15-20 says:

He is the image of the invisible God, the firstborn of all creation. For by him all things were created, in heaven and on earth, visible and invisible, whether thrones or dominions or rulers or authorities—all things were created through him and for him. And he is before all things, and in him all things hold together. And he is the head of the body, the church. He is the beginning, the firstborn from the dead, that in everything he might be preeminent. For in him all the fullness of God was pleased to dwell, and through him to reconcile to himself all things, whether on earth or in heaven, making peace by the blood of his cross.

And later Paul writes in Colossians 2:13-15, *"And you, who were dead in your trespasses and the uncircumcision of your flesh, God made alive together with him, having forgiven us all our trespasses, by canceling the record of debt that stood against us with its legal demands. This he set aside, nailing it to the cross. He disarmed the rulers and authorities and put them to open shame, by triumphing over them in him."*

What does it mean for us today to serve the High King in whom all authority and kindness dwells? What would life look like if we would submit ourselves to his authority completely? All of creation answers to his name. All of humanity will one day bow before him. But what would your life look like if you made the decision today to willfully lay down your life in response to his lordship? What would it look like to crown him as King of your plans, efforts, emotions, relationships, finances, past present, and future? You were not created to be the king of your own life. You were not created to bear the burden of doing life apart from the lordship of Jesus Christ. And you will never know true peace, joy, purpose, and love until you submit all you are to all God is.

Take time in guided prayer to meditate on the authority and power of Jesus. Thank him for his loving sacrifice and crown him King of your life today.

13

GUIDED PRAYER

1. Meditate on the authority and power of Jesus.
Allow Scripture to call you to a lifestyle of obedience and worship.

"Father, the hour has come; glorify your Son that the Son may glorify you, since you have given him authority over all flesh, to give eternal life to all whom you have given him." John 17:1-2

"On his robe and on his thigh he has a name written, King of kings and Lord of lords." Revelation 19:16

"He is the image of the invisible God, the firstborn of all creation. For by him all things were created, in heaven and on earth, visible and invisible, whether thrones or dominions or rulers or authorities—all things were created through him and for him. And he is before all things, and in him all things hold together. And he is the head of the body, the church. He is the beginning, the firstborn from the dead, that in everything he might be preeminent. For in him all the fullness of God was pleased to dwell, and through him to reconcile to himself all things, whether on earth or in heaven, making peace by the blood of his cross." Colossians 1:15-20

2. Thank Jesus for his sacrifice. Reflect on the depth of God's grace and power as demonstrated by the sacrifice of Jesus. God considers restored relationship with you worth the death of his perfect, only Son.

"And you, who were dead in your trespasses and the uncircumcision of your flesh, God made alive together with him, having forgiven us all our trespasses, by canceling the record of debt that stood against us with its legal demands. This he set aside, nailing it to the cross. He disarmed the rulers and authorities and put them to open shame, by triumphing over them in him." Colossians 2:13-15

"Worthy are you, our Lord and God, to receive glory and honor and power, for you created all things, and by your will they existed and were created." Revelation 4:11

"For God so loved the world, that he gave his only Son, that whoever believes in him should not perish but have eternal life." John 3:16

3. Crown Jesus as Lord of your life. Commit to surrendering everything to him today. Hand over control of your plans, relationships, finances, and emotions to the one who will guide you daily into the abundant life he died to give you.

"I came that they may have life and have it abundantly." John 10:10

"I know, O Lord, that the way of man is not in himself, that it is not in man who walks to direct his steps." Jeremiah 10:23

"I appeal to you therefore, brothers, by the mercies of God, to present your bodies as a living sacrifice, holy and acceptable to God, which is your spiritual worship." Romans 12:1

To take authority over your own life is to pluck yourself out of a life filled with the unimaginable graces of God. God will not bless that which is not his will. He waits patiently day after day for us to simply choose to submit ourselves to him and follow. He longs for the day when we will stop submitting to our own pride, yield ourselves to him, and discover the wealth of life available to us in him alone. May you have the courage and humility to surrender to God and follow him today.

Extended Reading: Colossians 3

Hope in
Relationship

DAY 2

DEVOTIONAL

In John 17:3, Jesus states one of the most important and direct truths in all of his High Priestly Prayer. Jesus says, *"And this is eternal life, that they know you the only true God, and Jesus Christ whom you have sent."* Eternal life is knowing God intimately—not just knowing about God, knowing of God, or knowing others who know God, but truly knowing him yourself.

"And this is eternal life, that they know you the only true God, and Jesus Christ whom you have sent."

JOHN 17:3

To be clear, consistently meeting with God directly is not a prerequisite for salvation. I can confidently say that I was saved as a young child, but it took years for me to discover the wealth of relationship available to me through Jesus. I went to church, heard about God, served him, and tried to live according to biblical principles, but I didn't really know the God I was spending so many hours devoted to. I hadn't really received his love for me. I hadn't experienced the peace and joy of his presence. I hadn't felt him speak to me or guide me directly. I wasn't experiencing the abundant life that only comes from personal, intimate relationship with my Father.

The truth is that God longs to be known by you. Jesus didn't die for the sole purpose of getting you to heaven. He sacrificed his life that you might truly live while here on earth. You are created to intimately know the God who formed you, saved you, and sustains you. And you will never find lasting peace until your life becomes wrapped up in the reality of his nearness and love.

The hope for all of humanity rests in relationship with the *"only true God, and Jesus Christ whom [he] sent."* Nothing in your life will be set right or brought in line with the power of Christ's death until you know the living God. You will not experience transformation and freedom from the depravity that surrounds you until you've counted *"everything as loss because of the surpassing worth of knowing Christ Jesus [your] Lord"* (Philippians 3:8).

How deeply do you know your heavenly Father? How real is he in your life? What are you still using to fill the void that can only be satisfied in intimate relationship with Jesus? Come before your Father and surrender your past, present, and future. Ask him to guide you into a deeper revelation of his reality, nearness, and love.

Jeremiah 9:23-24 says, *"Let not the wise man boast in his wisdom, let not the mighty man boast in his might, let not the rich man boast in his riches, but let him who boasts boast in this, that he understands and knows me, that I am the Lord who practices steadfast love, justice, and righteousness in the earth. For in these things I delight, declares the Lord."* As you enter into guided prayer, spend time getting to know in greater depths the "steadfast love, justice, and righteousness" of your God.

17

GUIDED PRAYER

1. Meditate on the importance of knowing your heavenly Father intimately.

"And this is eternal life, that they know you the only true God, and Jesus Christ whom you have sent." John 17:3

"Let not the wise man boast in his wisdom, let not the mighty man boast in his might, let not the rich man boast in his riches, but let him who boasts boast in this, that he understands and knows me, that I am the Lord who practices steadfast love, justice, and righteousness in the earth. For in these things I delight, declares the Lord." Jeremiah 9:23-24

"I love those who love me, and those who seek me diligently find me." Proverbs 8:17

2. Ask God to make the reality of his presence and nearness known to you in these moments.

"You will seek me and find me, when you seek me with all your heart." Jeremiah 29:13

3. Spend time getting to know the person of Jesus. While you may not be able to see him with your physical eyes, he will open the eyes of your heart to see him and know him. If you give him the chance, he will make his nearness known to you.

"Having the eyes of your hearts enlightened, that you may know what is the hope to which he has called you, what are the riches of his glorious inheritance in the saints." Ephesians 1:18

As believers, we must learn to live by faith. It's through faith in the truth of God's word, that he is real and that he loves us, that we begin to experience the Christianity Jesus died to give us. Religion apart from relationship leads to spiritual mediocrity. Christ came to set us free from the bonds of the law. He came to usher in a new covenant of grace and intimacy with God rather than a religion of merely rules and regulations. May you grow daily in your pursuit of knowing the reality and love of your heavenly Father and Jesus whom he sent.

Extended Reading: Ephesians 1

Unity in Our God

DEVOTIONAL

We were created for unity with fellow believers. It's in the pursuit of unity that the bonds of selfishness and pride are often broken. It's in the surrender of opinion and selfish ambition that we find the abundant life that comes through sacrificial living. And most importantly, it's in unity that Jesus is most glorified.

Jesus says in John 17:10-11, *"All mine are yours, and yours are mine, and I am glorified in them. And I am no longer in the world, but they are in the world, and I am coming to you. Holy Father, keep them in your name, which you have given me, that they may be one, even as we are one."* Unity between two humans is

"All mine are yours, and yours are mine, and I am glorified in them. And I am no longer in the world, but they are in the world, and I am coming to you. Holy Father, keep them in your name, which you have given me, that they may be one, even as we are one."

JOHN 17:10-11

only truly possible by the working of the Holy Spirit. Apart from God dwelling and transforming man, we will never be able to live sacrificially with any level of consistency. It's for that reason that Jesus is so glorified through our unity. And it's for that reason that pursuing unity between believers is of the utmost importance.

What are we declaring to the world when we bicker, slander, and give up on unity with fellow believers? Why would the lost want anything to do with a group of dramatic, hateful, judgmental, and selfish Christians? Christ has charged us with the command to be his hands and feet. He's commanded us to make disciples. And our ministry is nothing without love. When we pursue our own pride and gain over unity, we are directly disobeying the commandments of Scripture. When we allow strife and pride to place barriers between us, we hurt the cause of Christ to which we are all called.

Scripture is clear in its command to pursue unity. Unity isn't a suggestion that we don't have to adhere to because people can be difficult. It's a command straight from God, and it's of the highest importance.

Ephesians 4:1-3 says, *"I therefore, a prisoner for the Lord, urge you to walk in a manner worthy of the calling to which you have been called, with all humility and gentleness, with patience, bearing with one another in love, eager to maintain the unity of the Spirit in the bond of peace."* Romans 12:16 says, *"Live in harmony with one another. Do not be haughty, but associate with the lowly. Never be wise in your own sight."* And 2 Corinthians 13:11 says, *"Finally, brothers, rejoice. Aim for restoration, comfort one another, agree with one another, live in peace; and the God of love and peace will be with you."*

You are called to be a carrier of peace. The Holy Spirit dwelling within you longs to make you a person who pursues restoration, comfort, agreement, and peace with fellow believers. He longs to fill you with love, honor, patience, and respect for the fellow believers he has placed in your midst. When you feel dissension arise within you, choose to serve your brother or sister out of reverence for God. Choose to pursue peace at all costs. And in doing so you will bring glory to Jesus and declare to the world the wonderful transformation that comes only through salvation in Jesus.

GUIDED PRAYER

1. Meditate on the importance of unity in the body of believers.

"All mine are yours, and yours are mine, and I am glorified in them. And I am no longer in the world, but they are in the world, and I am coming to you. Holy Father, keep them in your name, which you have given me, that they may be one, even as we are one." John 17:10-11

"I therefore, a prisoner for the Lord, urge you to walk in a manner worthy of the calling to which you have been called, with all humility and gentleness, with patience, bearing with one another in love, eager to maintain the unity of the Spirit in the bond of peace." Ephesians 4:1-3

"Finally, brothers, rejoice. Aim for restoration, comfort one another, agree with one another, live in peace; and the God of love and peace will be with you." 2 Corinthians 13:11

2. What is keeping you from pursuing unity with believers around you? What thoughts or perspectives keep you from loving other Christians well? What work does the Spirit want to do in you today to help you pursue unity?

3. Surrender any pride or negativity that is keeping you from pursuing unity. Ask the Lord to give you the courage to fight for peace and choose a life of sacrifice rather than selfish ambition.

Loving others always has to start with you. You can't expect others to change before you choose to love them. The Lord doesn't call us to wait for others to get their lives sorted out before we pursue unity. He's asking us to choose obedience to him by loving others even when they don't deserve it. Choose love today and discover the abundant life and purpose within unity between believers.

Extended Reading: Ephesians 4

23

The Joy of the Lord

DAY 4

DEVOTIONAL

Jesus came to bring about the fullness of joy in man. Often we see Christians who are not exhibiting a lifestyle of joy, and therefore we assume God is not a happy God. We see all the darkness that surrounds and assume that God is most often angry or sad. But in John 17:13 Jesus prayed to the Father, *"But now I am coming to you, and these things I speak in the world, that they may have my joy fulfilled in themselves."*

*"But now I am coming to you, and these
things I speak in the world, that they may
have my joy fulfilled in themselves."*

JOHN 17:13

Jesus' prayer in John 17:13 demonstrates two important, life-changing truths for you and me today. First, Jesus had joy. We could not have his joy fulfilled in us if he doesn't have joy to start with. And the whole of Scripture supports the truth that within God dwells the fullness of joy. Psalm 16:11 says, *"You make known to me the path of life; in your presence there is fullness of joy; at your right hand are pleasures forevermore."* And Galatians 5:22 tells us that joy is a fruit of the Spirit. The God whom you have been filled with at salvation longs to produce the fruit of joy in your life. He longs to make you a joyful person from the inside out, that your joy wouldn't be based on circumstances or the fleeting whims of the world.

Second, John 17 tells us that we can have the joy of Jesus for ourselves. The God of joy longs to fill you to overflowing with satisfaction and hope. He longs to make your joy abundant and transcendent of the good or bad around you. God is joyful because it's a part of his nature. And he longs for it to be the same with you.

Do you believe that God is a joyful god? Have you experienced how happy he is? Have you met with him and encountered the joy and peace in his heart toward you? Zephaniah 3:17 says, *"The Lord your God is in your midst, a mighty one who will save; he will rejoice over you with gladness; he will quiet you by his love; he will exult over you with loud singing."* God longs to meet with you today and fill you with joy to overflowing. In Romans 15:13 Paul prays, *"May the God of hope fill you with all joy and peace in believing, so that by the power of the Holy Spirit you may abound in hope."* Joy is available to you today as you believe. There is hope in the Holy Spirit.

Come to God today with all your cares and burdens. Lay them at his feet and allow him to fill you with peace and joy where only heaviness abounded. God longs to set you free from the burdens of anxiety. He longs to lead you to a life of happiness and freedom in the Spirit. As you enter into guided prayer, choose to commit to God anything that has been weighing you down. Come before him with faith that he will shepherd you to greener pastures as you offer him your heart and follow his guidance.

25

GUIDED PRAYER

1. Meditate on God's desire to fill you with the joy of Jesus.

"But now I am coming to you, and these things I speak in the world, that they may have my joy fulfilled in themselves." John 17:13

"But the fruit of the Spirit is love, joy, peace, patience, kindness, goodness, faithfulness, gentleness, self-control; against such things there is no law." Galatians 5:22-23

"The thief comes only to steal and kill and destroy. I came that they may have life and have it abundantly." John 10:10

2. Lay your burdens at the feet of God. What concern, problem, circumstance, or relationship has been weighing on you? What has been stealing your joy lately? Cast all your cares at the feet of your heavenly Father who loves you.

"Casting all your anxieties on him, because he cares for you." 1 Peter 5:7

3. Ask God to fill you with joy inexpressible. Ask him to reveal to you his joy, and to help you bear the fruit of his Spirit.

Oftentimes we allow ourselves to be continually downcast rather than fighting for the joy available to us in God. Joy is a vital part of the Christian life. We are not made to carry burdens that steal our joy and keep us from the abundant life Jesus died to give us. Psalm 16:6 says, *"The lines have fallen for me in pleasant places; indeed, I have a beautiful inheritance."* God has plans to lead you to a life filled with the fullness of joy. May you pursue all the wonders and blessings God has in store for you today through the powerful sacrifice of Jesus.

Extended Reading: Psalm 16

The Truth
of Sanctification

SCRIPTURE

"I have given them your word, and the world has hated them because they are not of the world, just as I am not of the world. I do not ask that you take them out of the world, but that you keep them from the evil one. They are not of the world, just as I am not of the world. Sanctify them in the truth; your word is truth. As you sent me into the world, so I have sent them into the world. And for their sake I consecrate myself, that they also may be sanctified in truth." John 17:14-19

DEVOTIONAL

There is a level of freedom from sin in Christ that most of us in the body have yet to reach. Jesus prayed in John 17:14-19,

I have given them your word, and the world has hated them because they are not of the world, just as I am not of the world. I do not ask that you take them out of the world, but that you keep them from the evil one. They are not of the world, just as I am not of the world.

Sanctify them in the truth; your word is truth. As you sent me into the world, so I have sent them into the world. And for their sake I consecrate myself, that they also may be sanctified in truth.

Jesus declares a truth about you and me that we have yet to walk in fully: that our sanctification is linked to his consecration. He declares that we are not of the world just as he is not, that he has sent us into the world as he was sent, and prays that we would be sanctified in the truth.

For too long we have sat idle with the incredible gift of freedom bought at the highest price by the blood of Christ and left it unwrapped and thereby not experienced. By the blood of Jesus, we are transformed from being of the world, or of the conditions and brokenness of the world, to being given a new nature and identity of righteousness and holiness. 2 Corinthians 5:17 says, *"Therefore, if anyone is in Christ, he is a new creation. The old has passed away; behold, the new has come."* And later in verse 21 Paul writes, *"For our sake he made him to be sin who knew no sin, so that in him we might become the righteousness of God."* The gift of holiness is yours to be continually unwrapped and experienced day after day. Your portion is righteousness and peace in the Holy Spirit, not the weight and consequences of this sin-wrought world.

So how do we open this incredible gift of holiness? How do we pursue sanctification? What does it mean to be sanctified in the truth? It starts with renewing our mind every day to the truth of our new nature in Christ. We will never be able to live righteously if we continually believe we are sinners by nature. Christ has given us a new nature and filled us with the Holy Spirit who offers us freedom from sin in the midst of every temptation. But unless we spend time in the secret place renewing our mind and allowing God's love to satisfy and transform us, righteousness will only ever be a lofty goal that feels unachievable.

Next, we must pursue obedience to the Holy Spirit every single time he guides us. 1 Thessalonians 4:3-8 says,

For this is the will of God, your sanctification: that you abstain from sexual immorality; that each one of you know how to control his own body in holiness and honor, not in the passion of lust like the Gentiles who do not know God; that no one transgress and wrong his brother in this matter, because the Lord is an avenger in all these things, as we told you beforehand and solemnly warned you. For God has not called us for impurity, but in holiness. Therefore whoever disregards this, disregards not man but God, who gives his Holy Spirit to you.

We must not disregard the leadership of the Holy Spirit toward purity. If you feel like you shouldn't watch a TV show or movie, then don't. If the Spirit takes away your peace about anything you are doing, follow his guidance. Whatever you are doing in that moment might not be sin, but it might lead you down a path to sin. Trust the guidance of the Spirit. Follow where his peace, presence, and word take you. And pursue obedience and freedom at all costs. May you experience sanctification in the truth today as you meditate and spend time fellowshipping with the Spirit in guided prayer.

29

GUIDED PRAYER

1. Meditate on the truth of Scripture about your righteousness. Allow God's word to transform the way you think about yourself and sin. Allow it to lay a foundation for your present pursuit of sanctification and break the bonds of past weaknesses and sin.

"Therefore, if anyone is in Christ, he is a new creation. The old has passed away; behold, the new has come." 2 Corinthians 5:17

"For freedom Christ has set us free; stand firm therefore, and do not submit again to a yoke of slavery." Galatians 5:1

"So if the Son sets you free, you will be free indeed." John 8:36

2. Ask for forgiveness for any sin you have in your life. Spend time receiving God's forgiveness and allow him to lay a foundation for righteousness. Ask him why you struggle with certain temptations. Ask him what the path to freedom is for you.

"If we confess our sins, he is faithful and just to forgive us our sins and to cleanse us from all unrighteousness." 1 John 1:9

"No temptation has overtaken you that is not common to man. God is faithful, and he will not let you be tempted beyond your ability, but with the temptation he will also provide the way of escape, that you may be able to endure it." 1 Corinthians 10:13

"Blessed is the man who remains steadfast under trial, for when he has stood the test he will receive the crown of life, which God

has promised to those who love him. Let no one say when he is tempted, 'I am being tempted by God,' for God cannot be tempted with evil, and he himself tempts no one. But each person is tempted when he is lured and enticed by his own desire. Then desire when it has conceived gives birth to sin, and sin when it is fully grown brings forth death. Do not be deceived, my beloved brothers."
James 1:12-16

3. Spend time resting in the presence of God. Allow his love to fill you up, satisfy you, and transform you. Take note of how much more satisfying the presence of God is than anything of the world.

"Repent therefore, and turn again, that your sins may be blotted out, that times of refreshing may come from the presence of the Lord, and that he may send the Christ appointed for you, Jesus." Acts 3:19-20

"But for me it is good to be near God; I have made the Lord God my refuge, that I may tell of all your works." Psalm 73:28

The God you serve loves you and longs to empower you and free you from every sin that entangles you to the brokenness of the world. Therefore, may you be filled with joy at the truth of who you are in Christ. May you pursue obedience and righteousness with fervor and devotion. And may you experience the abundant life available to you as you are continually sanctified in the truth.

Extended Reading: 1 Thessalonians 4

The Glory
of God in Man

DEVOTIONAL

As disciples of Jesus, we are being fashioned into his likeness that we might be reflections of his glory. Jesus prays in John 17:22-24,

The glory that you have given me I have given to them, that they may be one even as we are one, I in them and you in me, that they may become perfectly one, so that the world may know that you sent me and loved them even as you loved me. Father, I desire that they also, whom you have given me, may be with me where I am, to see my glory that you have given me because you loved me before the foundation of the world.

Through the power of Christ's death, we are now filled with his very Spirit who is working constantly to fashion us into Christians in the truest sense of the word. To be a Christian is literally to be *"a little Christ."* We are meant to be marked by similarity to the one whom we serve and love. Our lives are to be filled with his love. Our minds are to be transformed by his words. And our hearts are to be devoted to serving him alone.

2 Corinthians 3:18 says, *"And we all, with unveiled face, beholding the glory of the Lord, are being transformed into the same image from one degree of glory to another. For this comes from the Lord who is the Spirit."* Through the death of Jesus we can come before God with unveiled face. Jesus came to declare the truth about who our Father is and to clear the path to restored intimacy between humanity and our Creator. And as we devote our lives to seeking the face of our heavenly Father, we will naturally become like him.

"The glory that you have given me I have given to them, that they may be one even as we are one. I in them and you in me, that they may become perfectly one, so that the world may know that you sent me and loved them even as you loved me. Father, I desire that they also, whom you have given me, may be with me where I am, to see my glory that you have given me because you loved me before the foundation of the world."

JOHN 17:22-24

God's desire is that we would live with the same freedom, intimacy, power, authority, and good works as Jesus. He sent his Son to die that we might be clothed from the inside out with Christ himself, thereby affording us a new life, nature, and identity. You are not the person you were before salvation. When you were filled with the Spirit of God, you were filled with the very glory of God, the image of Christ engraved upon your heart.

And while this concept of becoming like Christ often sounds heady and theological, it couldn't be of greater practical importance. It couldn't be more vital for us to believe and pursue the life given to us by the grace of God. Being transformed into the image of Jesus has powerful and practical implications for you and me. When you spend time with the Father, he desires to love you with the love he has shown Christ, a tangible and transformational love. He longs to set you free from the bonds of worldliness and sin. He longs to empower you and lead you to a life of purpose, miracles, and good works filled with the love of God himself. And he longs to lead you to a destiny laid before you since the foundation of the world.

Take time to seek the face of God today. Come before him with unveiled face and allow him to reveal to you the imprint of Christ upon your heart. Allow the Spirit to show you the purpose for which you were created. And receive the love of God that has the power to transform you into the very image of Jesus Christ, your Lord and example.

GUIDED PRAYER

1. Meditate on God's glory given to you at salvation. Reflect on the importance and availability of living like Jesus.

"I have been crucified with Christ. It is no longer I who live, but Christ who lives in me. And the life I now live in the flesh I live by faith in the Son of God, who loved me and gave himself for me." Galatians 2:20

"The glory that you have given me I have given to them, that they may be one even as we are one, I in them and you in me, that they may become perfectly one, so that the world may know that you sent me and loved them even as you loved me. Father, I desire that they also, whom you have given me, may be with me where I am, to see my glory that you have given me because you loved me before the foundation of the world." John 17:22-24

"And we all, with unveiled face, beholding the glory of the Lord, are being transformed into the same image from one degree of glory to another. For this comes from the Lord who is the Spirit." 2 Corinthians 3:18

2. Ask the Holy Spirit to fill you afresh. Ask him to engrave upon your heart the love and image of Christ in new ways. Ask him to guide you into a direct encounter with Jesus that you might know him personally.

"And do not get drunk with wine, for that is dissipation, but be filled with the Spirit." Ephesians 5:18

3. Spend time allowing God to transform you, love you, and set you free. Ask him what in your life isn't like Jesus. As he reveals sin in your life, confess it and turn to Jesus as your model. Seek out a life like his today.

"For to this you have been called, because Christ also suffered for you, leaving you an example, so that you might follow in his steps." 1 Peter 2:21

The death of Christ has more powerful implications than you or I will ever know this side of heaven. God has truly paved the way for us to live a life of incredible abundance. He offers us a life greater than we will find in anything of the world. May you pursue all the wealth of relationship available to you by the blood of Jesus. May you be transformed into his reflection on the earth. And may others come to know him by the depth of his love in you.

Extended Reading: 2 Corinthians 3

The Depth of God's Love for Us

DEVOTIONAL

There is no force more powerful than the love our heavenly Father has for us, his children. His love can move mountains, stop the roaring seas, heal broken bones and wounded hearts, transform lives, and set free those held captive by sin and shame. So great is his love for you and me that he sent his only Son

"O righteous Father, even though the world does not know you, I know you, and these know that you have sent me. I made known to them your name, and I will continue to make it known, that the love with which you have loved me may be in them, and I in them."

JOHN 17:25-26

to die that we might live through him. And in John 17:25-26, Jesus makes an unfathomable statement about how great the depth of God's love is for us:

O righteous Father, even though the world does not know you, I know you, and these know that you have sent me. I made known to them your name, and I will continue to make it known, that the love with which you have loved me may be in them, and I in them.

Do you know that God loves you the way he loves Jesus? His heart is full of affection for you. Jesus always prays perfectly in line with the will of the Father because they are one. So when Jesus prays for God to love us with the same love he has been given, his prayer is in perfect alignment with the heart of our Father.

Romans 8:37-39 says, *"No, in all these things we are more than conquerors through him who loved us. For I am sure that neither death nor life, nor angels nor rulers, nor things present nor things to come, nor powers, nor height nor depth, nor anything else in all creation, will be able to separate us from the love of God in Christ Jesus our Lord."* Through the death of Christ, the barrier between us and relationship with God was torn in two. The wrath of God was satisfied with Jesus' death, and now we can experience the full depth of

his love. Through Christ, we have been made new so that we can finally walk in unhindered fellowship and oneness with a holy, perfect God.

God loves you simply because he loves you. You don't have to work for his affection. You don't have to set yourself straight before God can pour out his love over you. The father in the prodigal son story ran out to meet his son before anything had ever been set right. He didn't know his son was there to apologize. He didn't care. He simply wanted to love his child. Your heavenly Father feels the same way about you. He longs to love you right where you are, as you are. He longs to fill you with love to overflowing. He longs for us to experience this love and oneness just as Jesus did when he walked the earth.

As you enter into guided prayer, open up your heart and allow God's grace to settle in. Allow him to free you from works-based religion and guide you to a lifestyle of relationship. God is not an angry taskmaster who shows affection only when you succeed. He is a loving Father who will always love you no matter what. Take time to receive the depth of his love for you today. Allow his love to heal you, transform you, free you, and lead you to the abundant life he has always longed to give.

37

GUIDED PRAYER

1. Meditate on the depth of God's love for you.

"In this the love of God was made manifest among us, that God sent his only Son into the world, so that we might live through him. In this is love, not that we have loved God but that he loved us and sent his Son to be the propitiation for our sins." 1 John 4:9-10

"No, in all these things we are more than conquerors through him who loved us. For I am sure that neither death nor life, nor angels nor rulers, nor things present nor things to come, nor powers, nor height nor depth, nor anything else in all creation, will be able to separate us from the love of God in Christ Jesus our Lord." Romans 8:37-39

"So we have come to know and to believe the love that God has for us. God is love, and whoever abides in love abides in God, and God abides in him." 1 John 4:16

2. Where do you need a fresh revelation of God's grace today? What's keeping you from receiving the depth of God's love? In what ways do you need him to show you how good of a Father he truly is?

3. Ask the Spirit to give you a revelation of God's grace and love for you. Receive God's presence and rest in his love. Meditate on and renew your mind to how deeply your heavenly Father loves you.

"Let us then with confidence draw near to the throne of grace, that we may receive mercy and find grace to help in time of need." Hebrews 4:16

"So that you may be sons of your Father who is in heaven. For he makes his sun rise on the evil and on the good, and sends rain on the just and on the unjust." Matthew 5:45

May the whole of Jesus' High Priestly Prayer be true in your life. May you come into the fullness of what Jesus died to give you. May your life be a wonderful reflection of his love. And may you experience the depth of his love for you in every season. You are a child of the Most High, loving God. He will never leave you nor forsake you. His love is powerful, real, and available. May your day be full of joy, peace, and purpose in light of God's glorious grace.

Extended Reading: Romans 8

Jesus our King

*"For to us a child is born, to us
a son is given." Isaiah 9:6*

WEEKLY OVERVIEW

What a gift we have in the Christmas season. God himself took on flesh and dwelt among us that we might find eternal relationship in him. His coming serves as a continual reminder of his grace and pursuit of us who are lost without him. As we look to Jesus this week to celebrate who he is and what he's done, may you find life-giving hope and foundational joy.

The Sacrificial King

DEVOTIONAL

It's impossible to separate the birth of Christ from the purpose of his coming. John 3:16 tells us, *"For God so loved the world, that he gave his only Son, that whoever believes in him should not perish but have eternal life."* As we take time today to look at the heart of a God who would sacrifice his own life that we might find life through him, let's open our hearts to receive a fresh encounter with his real, available love.

> *"Behold, the Lamb of God, who*
> *takes away the sin of the world!"*

JOHN 1:29

Jesus' coming was entirely a love-motivated decision— *"For God so loved the world."* So great is the depth of his love for his wayward crown of creation that he became man himself to live the life none of us ever could. So vast is his affection for us that he took the pain and shame we were due and offered up his life as a ransom for ours. Truly there is no greater love than the sacrifice of our King.

Have you stopped recently to acknowledge how intentionally God pursues you? Have you stopped to marvel at the lengths to which he will go simply to have your heart? In the hustle and bustle of this Christmas season, may we not look past the greatest gift we have. May we not skip over the reality of God's love for us to get to the next thing on the calendar. Instead, may we take time every day to let sink in the simple truth that God became man entirely for our sakes. God himself, who has no beginning, no limit, no weakness, and deserves no pain, took on flesh in pursuit of a deeper, richer, and entirely restored relationship with you and me.

The love of Jesus we celebrate at Christmastime is a sacrificial love. He didn't just give himself sacrificially on the cross. Every day of his life was another day given up for our sakes. Every tear, pang of hunger, and wound he suffered throughout his life he experienced not because he had to, but because he chose to out of love for us. Imagine leaving the perfection of heaven to come to earth. Imagine leaving unhindered, face-to-face connection with the heavenly Father and becoming an infant. Imagine allowing a mother and father to take care of you when you are God himself whose very existence has never known a beginning.

In this season of celebration may we take time to remember the loving, life-giving sacrifice of the King we worship. May we center our hearts and lives around him. May we give him the adoration and praise he deserves. And may this Christmas season change our lives forever as we respond to the continual pursuit of our loving God by offering him our hearts in return.

47

GUIDED PRAYER

1. Take a moment to reflect on the love of God reflected in the coming of Christ.

"For God so loved the world, that he gave his only Son, that whoever believes in him should not perish but have eternal life." John 3:16

2. Ask God to reveal all the ways in which he has been pursuing you lately. Allow the coming of Jesus to build your faith that God pursues you still.

3. Take time to respond to God's pursuit by offering him your heart. Crown him King of your life that all you are and have might be his. Commit to living today in response to God's great love for you.

"Let us go to his dwelling place; let us worship at his footstool!" Psalm 132:7

In Philippians 3:12 Paul writes, *"Not that I have already obtained this or am already perfect, but I press on to make it my own, because Christ Jesus has made me his own."* As a believer, Christ has made you his own. You were bought with a price only Jesus could pay. May this season be marked by the love and joy that can only come from true communion with Jesus, our sacrificial King.

Extended Reading: John 3

The King of Kings

DEVOTIONAL

The fate of so many nations has historically rested on the strength of its leaders. From Genghis Khan and Alexander the Great to King David, we look to kings as the catalyst for either victory or defeat, success or failure.

"On his robe and on his thigh he has a name written, King of kings and Lord of lords."

REVELATION 19:16

Scripture tells us in Revelation 19:16 that we as the people of God find our fate in the One True King. Scripture says, *"On his robe and on his thigh he has a name written, King of kings and Lord of lords."* Isaiah 9:6-7 says,

For to us a child is born, to us a son is given; and the government shall be upon his shoulder, and his name shall be called Wonderful Counselor, Mighty God, Everlasting Father, Prince of Peace. Of the increase of his government and of peace there will be no end, on the throne of David and over his kingdom, to establish it and to uphold it with justice and with righteousness from this time forth and forevermore. The zeal of the Lord of hosts will do this.

This Christmas season we celebrate the truth that our lives are hidden in Christ (Colossians 3:3). Our fate is wrapped up in his. Our victory and success is assured because our King sits enthroned on the heavens. He is high and lifted up, and his heart is filled with steadfast love for us, his bride.

If your future feels uncertain, if your heart is filled with anxiety, look no further than your Savior on whose robe and thigh is written, *"King of kings and Lord of lords."* If the furthest thing from your heart seems to be peace, look to Jesus, whom Scripture calls, *"Prince of Peace."* If you feel heavy and burdened from the weight and weariness of this world, look to God, our *"Wonderful Counselor."*

God's desire is to be near to you this season. His purpose is to pull you in closely to him and remind you that you are his and he will never let you go. Sometimes all we need to get through the day is a little perspective. Sometimes all we need to experience victory over our current circumstances is to remember that Jesus has already won us.

Take time today to bring your cares and weights to the feet of the *"King of kings."* Allow him to declare over you both his unceasing affection and limitless power. May you find abundant peace today in the person of Jesus.

GUIDED PRAYER

1. Meditate on what Scripture says about your Savior.

"On his robe and on his thigh he has a name written, King of kings and Lord of lords." Revelation 19:16

"The thief comes only to steal and kill and destroy. I came that they may have life and have it abundantly." John 10:10

2. What cares are weighing you down today?

What's keeping you from the abundant life Jesus came to bring you?

3. Bring your cares to Jesus in prayer. Ask him for a revelation of who you are in him. Take time to rest in his steadfast love and nearness.

"Humble yourselves, therefore, under the mighty hand of God so that at the proper time he may exalt you, casting all your anxieties on him, because he cares for you." 1 Peter 5:6-7

You and I are made to look to someone or something for leadership. We aren't created to rule our own lives. If we don't look to Jesus, we will undoubtedly look to this world, which only has the power to lead us away from abundant life in God. Where are your eyes set today? What are you looking to for provision, peace, and life? Fix your eyes on Jesus today, the *"founder and perfecter"* of our faith, that you might find transcendent peace and steadfast hope (Hebrews 12:2). May your day be filled with all the goodness of one who serves the *"King of kings."*

Extended Reading: Revelation 19

The Savior King

DEVOTIONAL

Sometimes as believers we've known Jesus to be our Savior for so long that we fail to dive in to all it means for us and thereby miss out on all the wonderful fruit salvation is meant to bear in our lives.

*"But God's firm foundation stands, bearing this seal:
'The Lord knows those who are his,' and, 'Let everyone
who names the name of the Lord depart from iniquity.'"*

2 TIMOTHY 2:19

Jesus died, not just to usher us into heaven at our death, but that we might find salvation from the things of this life that don't flow from the heart and hands of the Father. God's will is that we would walk in fullness of life all the days of our life (John 10:10). He has peace for us instead of anxiety (2 Thessalonians 3:16). He has an eternal purpose for us instead of frivolous pursuits (Ephesians 2:10). He longs to fill our hands with good gifts instead of the fruit of anxious toil (James 1:17). And he has a new nature and newness of life instead of the sins and cares of who we were before Christ (2 Corinthians 5:17).

So the questions in response to God's truth become: what are you waiting for? What's holding you back from all of these amazing things God has for you? What's keeping you from walking in newness of life today?

Experiencing the fruit of salvation begins with a clear revelation of what God does and doesn't want for you. Without faith to hold on to the promises of God, we easily fall victim to the lies and temptations of the enemy. Now that Satan has no hold over our eternal destiny, his pursuit is robbing us of all that's available to us in God that he might both hurt us and the heart of God.

But we serve a King who was not only Savior on the day of Calvary, but comes to us each day offering us salvation from the things of the world. The Holy Spirit inside each of us has the will and ability to deliver us from anything not found in the will of God that Jesus' sacrifice might bear its full fruit in our lives. And in spending time in dedicated communion with God, studying the Scripture to find what's been allotted as our portion in Jesus, and seeking to follow the moment-to-moment leadership of the Holy Spirit, we find the power we need to experience all God has for us.

Seek today to understand God's heart for you. Look for promises you can hold on to about his character and will. And in response to a revelation of God's will, have faith and vision to follow the leadership of the Holy Spirit into fullness of life. May today be marked by the life-giving fruit of salvation in Jesus.

55

GUIDED PRAYER

1. Meditate on the life available to you through salvation in Jesus.

"For 'In him we live and move and have our being'; as even some of your own poets have said, 'For we are indeed his offspring.'" Acts 17:28

"Behold, I stand at the door and knock. If anyone hears my voice and opens the door, I will come in to him and eat with him, and he with me." Revelation 3:20

"The thief comes only to steal and kill and destroy. I came that they may have life and have it abundantly." John 10:10

2. Spend time looking at your own life with the Holy Spirit. What in your life isn't in God's heart for you? Where are you not experiencing the fruit of salvation in Jesus?

"For who knows a person's thoughts except the spirit of that person, which is in him? So also no one comprehends the thoughts of God except the Spirit of God. Now we have received not the spirit of the world, but the Spirit who is from God, that we might understand the things freely given us by God." 1 Corinthians 2:11-12

3. Bring to God the parts of your life that aren't in his perfect will. Allow him to cast vision over your life. Let him fill you with faith to live the life he longs to give you.

"When the Spirit of truth comes, he will guide you into all the truth, for he will not speak on his own authority, but whatever he hears he will speak, and he will declare to you the things that are to come." John 16:13

"For I know the plans I have for you, declares the Lord, plans for welfare and not for evil, to give you a future and a hope." Jeremiah 29:11

God is a god of the journey. He doesn't expect perfection from us. He knows we are dust. He's just after your heart that you might go through this life together. Don't miss out on opportunities for relationship by running from the heart of God when you realize your own imperfection. Don't miss out on an opportunity to experience grace by trying to hide your sin. Allow God into everything you are and do. Journey with him that you might experience the wonders of a god who loves you just as you are. Find joy in experiencing right now the eternal relationship afforded you by your Savior King.

Extended Reading: 2 Corinthians 5

The Triumphant King

DEVOTIONAL

In Zechariah 9:9 we find a profound prophecy about Jesus, our triumphant King. Scripture says,

Rejoice greatly, O daughter of Zion! Shout aloud, O daughter of Jerusalem! Behold, your king is coming to you; righteous and having salvation is he, humble and mounted on a donkey, on a colt, the foal of a donkey.

"Fear not, daughter of Zion; behold, your king is coming, sitting on a donkey's colt!"

JOHN 12:15

Jesus achieved what no other king could have possibly accomplished, and he did it by taking the untrodden path of humility unto death. Jesus triumphed over death, ushered in salvation to all, and changed the eternal fate of the world through sacrifice. We serve a God who conquers with love.

Let us not miss the power in the metaphor Scripture prophesied and what it means for our lives today. When Jesus could have chosen any vessel to carry him down the pathway to victory, he chose a donkey. In a world where those who conquered rode horses and chariots, he chose a lowly foal. And after being mocked and beaten by the very ones he would offer victory, he chose the vessel of a cross as the means of triumph. He chose the final cry of death as a declaration of eternal life for all.

And in Jesus we find life by walking where he walked. Our triumph comes through a death of our own. Jesus says in Luke 9:23, *"If anyone would come after me, let him deny himself and take up his cross daily and follow me."* Paul says in Galatians 2:20, *"I have been crucified with Christ. It is no longer I who live, but Christ who lives in me. And the life I now live in the flesh I live by faith in the Son of God, who loved me and gave himself for me."*

Whatever victory you need today, you'll find it by laying down your own life and looking to your triumphant King. Freedom from sin comes from bringing who we are to the cross, engaging in authentic repentance, and discovering a new self won for us by Jesus' powerful death. Wisdom and vision come from laying down our own thoughts in humility and asking God, who gives *"generously to all"* (James 1:5). Abundant life is the fruit of all who triumph in continual death to self.

In what ways are you still looking to your own wisdom and strength to find victory? Where is pride getting in the way of triumph? Take time today as you enter into guided prayer to lay down your life that you might find it in Jesus.

59

GUIDED PRAYER

1. Meditate on the power of Jesus' triumphant sacrifice.

"For Christ also suffered once for sins, the righteous for the unrighteous, that he might bring us to God, being put to death in the flesh but made alive in the spirit." 1 Peter 3:18

"He himself bore our sins in his body on the tree, that we might die to sin and live to righteousness. By his wounds you have been healed." 1 Peter 2:24

2. Now reflect on Scripture's call to lay down your own life.

"If anyone would come after me, let him deny himself and take up his cross daily and follow me." Luke 9:23

"I have been crucified with Christ. It is no longer I who live, but Christ who lives in me. And the life I now live in the flesh I live by faith in the Son of God, who loved me and gave himself for me." Galatians 2:20

3. Bring to the cross anything in your life that's rooted in self rather than God. Repent of those things and find forgiveness and freedom in Jesus. Allow God to empower you with his spirit.

"Repent therefore, and turn back, that your sins may be blotted out, that times of refreshing may come from the presence of the Lord." Acts 3:19-20

"Now to him who is able to do far more abundantly than all that we ask or think, according to the power at work within us." Ephesians 3:20

Colossians 1:11-12 says, *"May you be strengthened with all power, according to his glorious might, for all endurance and patience with joy, giving thanks to the Father, who has qualified you to share in the inheritance of the saints in light."* Great is our inheritance in God. Great is the life won for us by Jesus. May you find power, strength, endurance, patience, and joy today as you look to Jesus, your triumphant king.

Extended Reading: Colossians 1

The Merciful King

DEVOTIONAL

The ministry of Jesus is laden with acts of mercy.
From acts of healing and forgiveness to meals shared
with those entirely undeserving of his attention, his
heart was filled with mercy for his people.

"Go and learn what this means, 'I desire
mercy, and not sacrifice.' For I came not to
call the righteous, but sinners."

MATTHEW 9:13

Have you ever thought that God might delight in showing you mercy? Have you ever thought that he might actually enjoy stepping into your world and offering that which you are wholly unworthy of? Does a good father loathe the times he needs to step in and forgive a child? Does a good father always force his kids to toe the line of perfection and offer only harsh words when they inevitably fail?

The very coming of Christ was an act of mercy. We who were left to try and find relationship under the law discovered our inability to live up to God's standards. When left to live by our own strength, we quickly reveal ourselves to be made of dust. But Jesus' coming demonstrated a part of God's heart we still find hard to believe today. God's desire is to step into the lives of his children and offer compassion and forgiveness where there is only failure and guilt. His desire is to pick us up even after we've made a mess and comfort us, while at the same time empowering us to live differently. We serve a merciful King.

Psalm 103:2-4 says, *"Bless the Lord, O my soul, and forget not all his benefits, who forgives all your iniquity, who heals all your diseases, who redeems your life from the pit, who crowns you with steadfast love and mercy."* Jesus bore a crown of thorns that we might be crowned with his steadfast love and mercy. Jesus, the only one deserving of God's love, took on the guilt and shame we deserved that our lives might be marked by compassion and grace.

In this life you will make mistakes. There will not be a single day in which you experience perfection. But Jesus' birth, life, and death reveal to us that life is not about our imperfections but about God's perfect love. Life is not about our failures or successes but about the God who loves us through it all.

Take time today to allow God to crown you with his steadfast love and mercy that your heart might find peace in the arms of your merciful King.

63

GUIDED PRAYER

1. Meditate on the mercy of God. Allow Scripture to fill you with faith to receive what you do not deserve.

"The steadfast love of the Lord never ceases; his mercies never come to an end; they are new every morning; great is your faithfulness." Lamentations 3:22-23

"Bless the Lord, O my soul, and forget not all his benefits, who forgives all your iniquity, who heals all your diseases, who redeems your life from the pit, who crowns you with steadfast love and mercy." Psalm 103:2-4

2. Where do you need a revelation of God's mercy today? Where are you feeling frustration or guilt around your weaknesses?

3. Ask God for a revelation of his mercy. Ask him how he sees your weaknesses. Allow his mercy to lay a new foundation for your life that you might live by grace today.

"Let us then with confidence draw near to the throne of grace, that we may receive mercy and find grace to help in time of need." Hebrews 4:16

In Matthew 9:13 Jesus says, *"Go and learn what this means, 'I desire mercy, and not sacrifice.' For I came not to call the righteous, but sinners."* We are called to live as agents of God's mercy. One of the most powerful ways we can reflect the character of Jesus is by offering mercy to those in desperate need of it. Don't hold others to standards of perfection. Rather, show forgiveness and love to those who, like you, are in desperate need of grace. May you find joy in being used by God to bring light and love to others today.

Extended Reading: Psalm 103

The Just King

DEVOTIONAL

Often the word "justice" is taken as synonymous with punishment. Our societies have justice systems. We demand justice for the oppressed by punishing the wrongdoer. We see justice as the necessary counter to our world's inherent depravity.

"Therefore the Lord waits to be gracious to you, and therefore he exalts himself to show mercy to you. For the Lord is a God of justice; blessed are all those who wait for him."

ISAIAH 30:18

To be sure, justice is an incredibly important component to life. But we serve a King who, while entirely just, is also completely merciful. We serve a God who doesn't shy away from consequence and conviction but looks for every opportunity to give good gifts to his children.

Isaiah 30:18 illustrates this heavenly tension in saying, *"Therefore the Lord waits to be gracious to you, and therefore he exalts himself to show mercy to you. For the Lord is a God of justice; blessed are all those who wait for him."* Isaiah spoke this word to an incredibly idolatrous people. Israel was not a nation we would judge as worthy of blessing. But God, through his heart of mercy and justice, constantly led his people back into his fold by whatever means necessary that he might reward them with good and pleasing gifts.

Even in moments of weakness your heavenly Father loves you. Even in moments where you would condemn yourself your Father delights in showing mercy. And even though we don't deserve one good thing from a perfect God, because of his merciful justice he lavishly rewards even the smallest of good within us.

James 1:17 teaches us, *"Every good gift and every perfect gift is from above, coming down from the Father of lights with whom there is no variation or shadow due to change."* All that is good in your life was supplied by the hand of your heavenly Father. Every dollar you've made and possession you've received was God's good pleasure to give you. Every friendship you've developed and family member added to your number was graciously provided to you because you serve a just and merciful King.

In this Christmas season may we celebrate the just heart of Jesus. May we find peace and comfort in the fact that God sees the world rightly but looks upon us with compassion. And may our hearts be filled with worship as we look to Jesus, our just King.

GUIDED PRAYER

1. Meditate on the just heart of Jesus. Allow the truth of God's character to open up places in your heart to receive him.

"Therefore the Lord waits to be gracious to you, and therefore he exalts himself to show mercy to you. For the Lord is a God of justice; blessed are all those who wait for him." Isaiah 30:18

2. Where do you see the merciful justice of God in your life? Where do you see him bestowing gifts upon you?

"Every good gift and every perfect gift is from above, coming down from the Father of lights with whom there is no variation or shadow due to change." James 1:17

3. Take time to worship Jesus in response to everything he's given you. Offer up prayers of thanksgiving to him for all his goodness.

"Sing praises to the Lord, for he has done gloriously; let this be made known in all the earth." Isaiah 12:5

Part of the mystery of the Christian life is embracing paradoxes. We serve a God of mercy and justice. We who deserve nothing have been given everything. Life with God is filled with glorious paradox. May we celebrate who God is this season and offer him our hearts in response to his great love. May we elevate the King of justice who in his loving-kindness took on flesh that he might get the punishment we deserved. All glory to Jesus, our just King.

Extended Reading: Isaiah 30

The Humble King

DEVOTIONAL

There has never been a greater depth of humility than what we find in Jesus. He was a man marked by astonishing sacrifice. He lived in utter devotion to God the Father and us, his undeserving people. Philippians 2:5-7 says, *"Have this mind among yourselves, which is yours in Christ Jesus, who, though he was in the form of God, did not count equality with God a thing to be grasped, but emptied himself, by taking the form of a servant, being born in the likeness of men."*

"Have this mind among yourselves, which is yours in Christ Jesus, who, though he was in the form of God, did not count equality with God a thing to be grasped, but emptied himself, by taking the form of a servant, being born in the likeness of men."

PHILIPPIANS 2:5-7

Jesus became a servant so we could be made sons and daughters. He took on flesh that our flesh might find true redemption. He emptied himself of that which he was rightfully owed that we might receive grace upon grace, which we've done nothing to deserve.

The coming of Christ we celebrate at Christmas is entirely descriptive of the heart of God. Just as Jesus came to make a way for us, he comes still. Just as Jesus came that fateful day millennia ago, he comes to meet with us still. And just as the world received its greatest gift in Jesus, we still find in the presence of God our greatest gift on a daily basis.

We can find hope and joy in the fact that we serve a humble King. Our King does nothing from selfish ambition. Unlike us, he does nothing to better himself or cover for his own inadequacies. Rather, because he is already entirely full and complete, he gives of himself freely that we might live in the light of his grace and love. He doesn't use his deity to demand anything from us, but instead to give us life, breath, and meaning.

Take time today to rest in the humility of Jesus. Find hope for your past, present, and future in the simple truth that Jesus has and will continue to be everything you need. And open your heart to receive the life-giving presence of your humble King.

GUIDED PRAYER

1. Meditate on the humility of Jesus. Allow Scripture to paint a clear picture of the heart of God.

"Have this mind among yourselves, which is yours in Christ Jesus, who, though he was in the form of God, did not count equality with God a thing to be grasped, but emptied himself, by taking the form of a servant, being born in the likeness of men." Philippians 2:5-7

2. Choose to trust in the humble leadership of God. Give him every part of your life knowing that he doesn't lead you out of selfish motive, but leads you entirely for your good.

"I am the good shepherd. The good shepherd lays down his life for the sheep." John 10:11

"The Lord is my shepherd; I shall not want." Psalm 23:1

3. Take time to rest in the presence of Jesus. Receive the gift of his nearness. Find joy in the depth of his love.

"My presence will go with you, and I will give you rest." Exodus 33:14

Philippians 2:9-11 illustrates a truth of the kingdom we as believers need to know:

Therefore God has highly exalted him and bestowed on him the name that is above every name, so that at the name of Jesus every knee should bow, in heaven and on earth and under the earth, and every tongue confess that Jesus Christ is Lord, to the glory of God the Father.

Jesus is the perfect example of the truth that *"everyone who exalts himself will be humbled, and he who humbles himself will be exalted"* (Luke 14:11). The pathway to life in God is humility. When you seek to serve the Father and others as Jesus did, you will discover a wellspring of joy and life not found in prideful pursuits. Seek to live in humility today and find unfathomable grace and love in Jesus, your humble King.

Extended Reading: Philippians 2

Drawing near

"Draw near to God, and he will draw near to you." James 4:8

WEEKLY OVERVIEW

The Christmas season is a powerful and unique time of year to remember that Jesus came to make a way for us to be near God. In his life, death, and resurrection, Jesus built a bridge between us and God allowing us to have continual, unhindered communion with our Creator. But God can't force us into nearness with him. Even as believers filled with the Holy Spirit, we can choose to live as if God is still far off. So this Christmas season, may we choose to open our hearts to the living God that we might experience fullness of joy in his loving presence.

The Importance of Drawing Near

DEVOTIONAL

James 4:8 contains a profound promise of God. Scripture says, *"Draw near to God, and he will draw near to you."* For a while I thought this verse seemed backwards. Doesn't God do the drawing? Isn't God the one who's constantly pursuing us?

After diving deeper into the meaning of James 4:8 I discovered an important truth that's foundational to living in communion with God: the door of God's heart is always open to us. His love is always for us. His presence is always available. The Father

*"Draw near to God, and he
will draw near to you."*

JAMES 4:8

turned away from Jesus as ours sins rested squarely on his shoulders ensuring he would never have to turn away from us.

To draw near to God is to simply open our hearts to what was always available. It's not that God ever withholds his presence from us. It's that he never forces us to abide in him. If we want to go our own way, he willingly and patiently waits for us. And the moment that we turn our hearts back to him, he is there to fill us with a revelation of his loving nearness and unwavering devotion.

In his book, *The Pursuit of God*, A. W. Tozer describes two veils. The first veil was the veil between the Holy of Holies and the world that was torn at the death of Jesus, signifying the availability of God's manifest presence to all. The second veil is the veil of our own hearts that's our decision to tear by God's grace.

Whether it's the effects of sin and shame or a lack of understanding what's available to us in Christ, all of us have the ability to veil places in our hearts. All of us can shield our beliefs about our identity, our

possessions, or our relationships from the abiding presence of Jesus and live apart from communion with him. We all have the ability at any given moment to go our own way and miss out on abundant life.

But the truth is that the Christian life isn't about our ability to abide in God perfectly, but about God's grace to draw near to us in response to repentance. God has no expectation that we would live this life perfectly. He remembers our frame and knows we are dust (Psalm 103:14). What he desires from us is to allow the Holy Spirit to illuminate any parts of our lives that aren't his that we would be quick to repent and enjoy his grace-filled presence once again. God is not angry with you for veiling your heart. He knows better than you do the reasons you aren't letting him fully in. His heart is filled with the fullness of compassion for you that you might live to experience his grace rather than strive and condemn yourself for your imperfection.

Take time today to rend the veil of your own heart, draw near to God, and experience the glory of his manifest presence.

GUIDED PRAYER

1. Meditate on God's promise to draw near to you if you will draw near to him. Allow the truth of God's word to fill you with faith to encounter God.

"Draw near to God, and he will draw near to you." James 4:8

"You will seek me and find me, when you seek me with all your heart." Jeremiah 29:13

2. What parts of your heart seem veiled today? Where are you going your own way? Where in your life are you not experiencing abundant life in God synonymous with communion with him?

3. Rend the veil over your own heart today and allow God to flood those places with his forgiveness and grace. Take time to allow him to fill you with a revelation of his love.

"We have this as a sure and steadfast anchor of the soul, a hope that enters into the inner place behind the curtain, where Jesus has gone as a forerunner on our behalf, having become a high priest forever after the order of Melchizedek." Hebrews 6:19-20

May Hebrews 10:19-22 provide joy and hope to your heart as you seek to draw near to your heavenly Father:

Therefore, brothers, since we have confidence to enter the holy places by the blood of Jesus, by the new and living way that he opened for us through the curtain, that is, through his flesh, and since we have a great priest over the house of God, let us draw near with a true heart in full assurance of faith, with our hearts sprinkled clean from an evil conscience and our bodies washed with pure water.

Extended Reading: Hebrews 10

Every Morning Is Like Christmas with God

DEVOTIONAL

As a child, Christmas morning was always the highlight of my year. I could hardly sleep the night before as I waited for the chance to open up the gifts my wonderful parents had purchased for me. It still makes me smile to remember the unbridled joy I felt at the sound of my alarm in the morning, feeling the expectation of what was to come.

"The steadfast love of the Lord never ceases; his mercies never come to an end; they are new every morning; great is your faithfulness."

LAMENTATIONS 3:22-23

James 1:17 tells us, *"Every good gift and every perfect gift is from above, coming down from the Father of lights with whom there is no variation or shadow due to change."* And Lamentations 3:22-23 says, *"The steadfast love of the Lord never ceases; his mercies never come to an end; they are new every morning; great is your faithfulness."*

Every morning with God can be like Christmas morning. From the moment our eyes open we have an opportunity to know a love that surpasses any gift we've been given. From the time our feet hit the ground we can experience perfect, pleasing plans the Lord has laid before us.

Every moment in our day is a chance to receive more and more grace and more and more love. Every encounter with a person is a chance to see God move and work through us and through them. Every task given us is a chance to experience the anointing and empowerment of the Holy Spirit. Even in trial and tribulations we are given an opportunity to experience a heavenly, eternal peace that transcends our circumstances. Even in pain and loss we are given a chance to experience the loving, compassionate heart of our Father that gets low with us and meets us where we are.

If we will allow it, God will turn every moment into a chance to experience the fullness of his love. If we will set our eyes on Jesus in faith and let him into every part of our hearts and days, we will live lives filled with the amazing gifts of a God with limitless resources.

May this Christmas season be a reminder that every day of the year is good with God. May the gifts we receive be a reminder that every good thing, both at Christmas and throughout our year, comes from the hands of our loving heavenly Father. And may we wake up each day in joyful expectation to experience the steadfast love of our ever-present Creator.

Take time in guided prayer to meditate on God's heart to give you good gifts and find rest in his life-giving presence.

85

GUIDED PRAYER

1. Meditate on the heart of God to give you good and perfect gifts.

"Every good gift and every perfect gift is from above, coming down from the Father of lights with whom there is no variation or shadow due to change." James 1:17

2. Spend some time opening your heart to receive the presence of God. Hand over to him anything that's weighing you down that you might experience merciful peace.

"The steadfast love of the Lord never ceases; his mercies never come to an end; they are new every morning; great is your faithfulness." Lamentations 3:22-23

3. Ask God for a revelation of the good gifts he has in store for you. Ask him to help you keep your focus on him today that you might have eyes to see all the ways he is blessing you.

"What no eye has seen, nor ear heard, nor the heart of man imagined, what God has prepared for those who love him." 1 Corinthians 2:9

May God grant you an eternal perspective today to see things as he does. May you have vision to see your circumstances and relationships in light of God's continued grace. May your heart grow increasingly soft today as you see God's abundant provision over you. And may the result of it all be unceasing prayers of thanksgiving that delight the heart of your heavenly Father.

Extended Reading: Psalm 30

God Does
the Drawing

DEVOTIONAL

The eyes of God are always set upon us. He looks
at us with a smile on his face and love in his heart.
Because of who he is—namely his nature of love—
he is in constant pursuit of us. His love never relents.

"We love because he first loved us."

1 JOHN 4:19

His grace is like an ever-flowing river making its way to replenish the earth and those who fill it. The only question that remains is, are we willing to dive in?

1 John 4:19 says in beautiful simplicity, *"We love because he first loved us."* If we have one iota of love in our hearts toward God it is because he has loved us first. If we have even an inkling of desire to seek after him, it is because he has sought after us every moment of our lives.

If your desire is to experience God, if you long to live in communion with him, you need look no further than the truth that he is pursuing you. To experience him is simply to let him in. To love him is simply to receive his love. Intimacy with God is as pure and simple as breathing.

In a world filled with complicated doctrines and strenuous programs it's time for the people of God to rest in the simplicity of God. Abundant life boils down to the truth that God is available. He never

leaves us or forsakes us (Hebrews 13:5). He never turns his heart away from us. But in love he draws us to himself knowing that the absolute best place for us is in his arms.

If you will choose to experience God—to respond to his drawing—know that the Holy Spirit is within you to help you. There is nothing in the way of you knowing the heart of God because God himself couldn't be any closer. The Holy Spirit can and will reveal how God feels and what God's saying if you'll ask. He will give you the eyes to see the Father drawing you close if you'll open your heart to him. And in response to his drawing he will show you how you can seek him in return.

Deuteronomy 4:29 says, *"But from there you will seek the Lord your God and you will find him, if you search after him with all your heart and with all your soul."* Take time in guided prayer today to respond to the drawing of the Lord by seeking after him with all you are and have.

GUIDED PRAYER

1. Meditate on the heart of God to draw you close to him.

"We love because he first loved us." 1 John 4:19

"Behold, I stand at the door and knock. If anyone hears my voice and opens the door, I will come in to him and eat with him, and he with me." Revelation 3:20

2. Ask the Holy Spirit to reveal God's heart for you. Pay attention to anything you hear, feel, or see. Trust that God longs to reveal his love to you.

"For the Spirit searches everything, even the depths of God." 1 Corinthians 2:10

3. Respond to the love of God by offering him your heart in return. Tell him that you love him. Tell him what you're thankful for. Spend time receiving and giving love that you might rest in intimacy with your Creator.

"The Lord is good to those who wait for him, to the soul who seeks him." Lamentations 3:25

"You have said, 'Seek my face.' My heart says to you, 'Your face, Lord, do I seek.'" Psalm 27:8

In *The Pursuit of God*, A. W. Tozer wrote, "God must do everything for us. Our part is to yield and trust." May you yield to the drawing of God today. May you find peace through trusting in his steadfast love. And may you discover more and more ways God has loved you from the first.

Extended Reading: Psalm 27

Sensitivity
in Busyness

DEVOTIONAL

In Ephesians 5:15-17 Paul writes, *"Look carefully then how you walk, not as unwise but as wise, making the best use of the time, because the days are evil. Therefore do not be foolish, but understand what the will of the Lord is."* Do you ever feel like your days are evil? Do you ever feel like the busyness of your life rules you?

*"Look carefully then how you walk, not as unwise
but as wise, making the best use of the time, because
the days are evil. Therefore do not be foolish, but
understand what the will of the Lord is."*

EPHESIANS 5:15-17

Society today loves busyness. We love to fill our plates to the brim and find purpose in what we're doing rather than why we're doing it. We speak ill of our own lives, as if we have no choice in the ways we spend our time. We talk about how church, work, family, and friends all pull from us as if the word "no" didn't exist. And the season of Christmas can be even worse! With finishing work up to be able to take time off and the stress of family, parties, and expectations, Christmas can be one of the busiest times of the year.

Maybe God would have you set better boundaries this season. Or maybe he would have you do everything you're doing. Only you and the Holy Spirit can know. But regardless of how busy you are, the key to walking in the joy and peace of God is sensitivity.

Even in the most rushed times of life, God is there, beckoning you to let him in to all your doing and feeling that you might do life with him. Even in difficult relationships and too much work, God has wisdom and truth for you that you might have a better perspective on life.

Through the power of the Spirit you can take ownership of your life. By God's grace you can walk wisely and make every moment a chance to see God's kingdom come both in your life and the lives of others. Your ears have been opened to the voice of God by the filling of the Spirit. Your nature as a believer is one filled and fed by the very presence of God. You have life within you, the glory of God manifest as the fruit of Jesus' sacrifice.

Take time today to hear the voice of God. Find God's heart that you might be sensitive to what he's saying and where he's leading, even in the busyness of today. May you find rest for your soul that transcends your circumstances as God fills your every moment with his loving-kindness.

GUIDED PRAYER

1. Meditate on the availability and importance of being sensitive to the Holy Spirit.

"Look carefully then how you walk, not as unwise but as wise, making the best use of the time, because the days are evil. Therefore do not be foolish, but understand what the will of the Lord is." Ephesians 5:15-17

2. What truth would God have you know today? What perspective would he give you on your life? Ask him for wisdom and vision. Take some time to listen to God.

"If any of you lacks wisdom, let him ask God, who gives generously to all without reproach, and it will be given him." James 1:5

3. Rest in the presence of God. Discover his nearness that you might stay connected to him throughout your day today.

"But for me it is good to be near God; I have made the Lord God my refuge, that I may tell of all your works." Psalm 73:28

God longs to be a refuge for you. He longs to be a shelter to which you can run when life overwhelms you from any and all fronts. He longs to speak peace over your heart when storms arise. He longs to wrap you up with wisdom and love that you might walk a path laid out before you by the leading of the Holy Spirit. Peace and joy are yours in the Spirit if you will grab hold of him today and trust him with all you are. May you be sensitive to who God is and all he's doing—even in the midst of busyness.

Extended Reading: Psalm 91

Solitude with Emmanuel

DEVOTIONAL

One of the greatest privileges of the Christian faith is solitude with God. Engaging in solitude with our Creator is a life-giving celebration of his heart. Our God isn't after what we can do for him. He's not after fixing us. He's all about having us. He's all about being with his people in restored, unhindered relationship.

*"And the Word became flesh and dwelt among us,
and we have seen his glory, glory as of the only Son
from the Father, full of grace and truth."*

JOHN 1:14

Isaiah 7:14 prophesies about the birth of Christ saying, *"Therefore the Lord himself will give you a sign. Behold, the virgin shall conceive and bear a son, and shall call his name Immanuel."* Immanuel means, "God with us." How amazing is it that the King of heaven and earth would desire to be called "God with us" and that our Creator would want to be known as one who would write himself into the story of his creation in such a way as to be tangibly, truly present.

When we take time to get alone with the Father apart from any other agenda, to simply open our hearts and be with him, we declare to ourselves and to God that our lives are centered around him. When we make space to hold off on questions (and reading, learning, and growing) to simply rest in his nearness, we discover that God is far better and far more loving than we ever could have guessed.

Solitude with God is a place of abundant joy. It's a place of peace and encounter that no other spiritual discipline can bring. It's a source of perspective and freedom in times typically marked by frivolous pursuits and stress. And it's a cornerstone of Christian spirituality: a pursuit of God that casts aside every ulterior motive to simply and purely be with God.

John 1:14 says, *"And the Word became flesh and dwelt among us, and we have seen his glory, glory as of the only Son from the Father, full of grace and truth."* The heart of Jesus is marked by grace and truth. He sees you as you are. He knows exactly what you need. Take time to discover the grace of God to speak to you as you simply open your heart and listen. Trust in his perfect love and leadership by sitting at his feet and letting him say everything, or nothing at all. Fix your eyes on Jesus today and enjoy the simplicity of solitude. May your heart be filled with peace and joy as you encounter Emmanuel, God with us.

GUIDED PRAYER

1. Begin a time of solitude by meditating on the availability of God's presence.

"Therefore the Lord himself will give you a sign. Behold, the virgin shall conceive and bear a son, and shall call his name Immanuel." Isaiah 7:14

"Where shall I go from your Spirit? Or where shall I flee from your presence? If I ascend to heaven, you are there! If I make my bed in Sheol, you are there!" Psalm 139:7-8

2. Take time to receive the presence of God. Sometimes it helps me to take deep breaths as a symbol for breathing in the presence of God and breathing out all my cares and weights.

"Then the Lord God formed the man of dust from the ground and breathed into his nostrils the breath of life, and the man became a living creature." Genesis 2:7

3. Rest in the nearness of Jesus. Decide not to ask questions or wonder about the things going on in your life. Instead, simply enjoy the goodness of God.

"And rising very early in the morning, while it was still dark, he departed and went out to a desolate place, and there he prayed." Mark 1:35

One of the greatest markers in my life for how I'm doing is how consistently I am getting time to simply enjoy God. Loving and being loved by God is foundational to every other aspect of the Christian life. It's only in experiencing God's love that I can effectively love others. It's only in enjoying God that I am able to fully enjoy family and friends. Sometimes the simplest of things are the most powerful. May your heart be light today as you find joy in the simplicity of solitude.

Extended Reading: Isaiah 7

Drawing from the Endless Well

DEVOTIONAL

In John 4:7-15 we find a powerful metaphor illustrating God's heart for his people:

A woman from Samaria came to draw water. Jesus said to her, "Give me a drink." (For his disciples had gone away into the city to buy food.) The Samaritan woman said to him, "How is it that you, a Jew, ask for a drink from me, a woman of Samaria?" (For Jews have no dealings with Samaritans.) Jesus answered her, "If you knew the gift of God, and who it is that is saying to you, Give me a drink, you would have asked him, and he would have given you living water." The woman said to him, "Sir, you have nothing to draw water with, and the well is deep. Where do you get that living water? Are you greater than our father Jacob? He gave us the well and drank from it himself, as did his sons and his livestock." Jesus said to her, "Everyone who drinks of this water will be thirsty again, but whoever drinks of the water that I will give him will never be thirsty again. The water that I will give him will become in him a spring of water welling up to eternal life." The woman said to him, "Sir, give me this water, so that I will not be thirsty or have to come here to draw water."

"If you knew the gift of God, and who it is that is saying to you, 'Give me a drink,' you would have asked him, and he would have given you living water."

JOHN 4:10

We were created with an insatiable thirst for relationship with God. We were made to experience true rest and satisfaction in one place and from one relationship: intimacy with the Father. In Jesus we find what our hearts have been looking for from our first breath. In Jesus we find a pathway to the Father not formed by our exploration or wandering, but by his steadfast love and unceasing pursuit.

Jesus looks to you and me today and offers us life-giving water that satiates our most foundational thirst. He places within us *"a spring of water welling up to eternal life."* He gives us clear, boundless access to intimacy with God that our hearts might overflow with rivers of his loving-kindness. And this love isn't something we have to strive for. It's not something we have to work to earn. Rather, it's a free gift, like salvation, that we can simply open our hearts to and receive.

Take time today to receive what God so freely gives. Find rest and purpose in intimacy with your Creator. Cease your striving and open your heart to the God who's loved you from the first. And drink deeply of the endless well of God's steadfast love.

GUIDED PRAYER

1. Meditate on God as your source of satisfaction and life.

"If you knew the gift of God, and who it is that is saying to you, 'Give me a drink,' you would have asked him, and he would have given you living water." John 4:10

"With joy you will draw water from the wells of salvation." Isaiah 12:3

2. Where do you need the life-giving waters of God's presence today? Where do you need him to fill you up that you might operate from a place of overflow?

"For I will pour water on the thirsty land, and streams on the dry ground; I will pour my Spirit upon your offspring, and my blessing on your descendants." Isaiah 44:3

3. Draw from the waters of God's love. Receive his presence and find rest for your soul in his steadfast love.

"He makes me lie down in green pastures. He leads me beside still waters. He restores my soul." Psalm 23:2-3

When we live as those fulfilled by God's goodness, we are positioned to see Heaven come to earth. Psalm 84:5-7 says,

Blessed are those whose strength is in you, in whose heart are the highways to Zion. As they go through the Valley of Baca they make it a place of springs; the early rain also covers it with pools. They go from strength to strength; each one appears before God in Zion.

The Valley of Baca was the driest place in the area. It wasn't a place marked by springs or early rain. But when God's people spend time following their hearts to his presence, or Zion, he makes what was dry and weary a place filled with life and health. He takes what was once desolate and makes it fertile and life-giving. Trust that as you spend time with the Lord he will make you an instrument of his kingdom. Trust that as your heart is transformed by his love that he will use you to transform the world around you. May you be a powerful instrument of renewal and redemption today as you live from a place of intimacy with your Creator.

Extended Reading: Psalm 84

Carrying the Presence of Christ

DAY 21

DEVOTIONAL

We have the privilege as Jesus' disciples of carrying his presence with us into the world. God in his love has chosen to use us as agents of awakening. He's commissioned us to *"Go therefore and make disciples of all nations, baptizing them in the name of the Father and of the Son and of the Holy Spirit"* (Matthew 28:19). And in 1 John 4:15-17 we gain an insight into the way in which God would have us make disciples:

"By this is love perfected with us, so that we may have confidence for the day of judgment, because as he is so also are we in this world."

1 JOHN 4:17

Whoever confesses that Jesus is the Son of God, God abides in him, and he in God. So we have come to know and to believe the love that God has for us. God is love, and whoever abides in love abides in God, and God abides in him. By this is love perfected with us, so that we may have confidence for the day of judgment, because as he is so also are we in this world.

"As he is so also are we in this world." What a powerful statement! God's plan for the world is to form and fashion us into those who reflect his goodness to others. The hope of the world rests in Jesus' mercy and grace as proclaimed through our lives. And the only way in which we carry Jesus with us into the world is by abiding in God and allowing him to abide in us.

Do you know that you can abide in God? And not just in spending time alone with him! 1 John 4 teaches us that when we abide in love, when we love others, we are abiding in him. You see, abiding in God requires us to be where he is. It requires us to yield to his leadership and heart that we might join him throughout our day where he is already at work. Sometimes abiding requires time spent in solitude, the word, and worship. Other times abiding requires action.

Where is God at work in your midst today? Who is he pursuing and how can you join him? Who is he drawing to himself and how can you help him? If you want to be with God today, join him in seeing his kingdom of love advance. If you want to abide in the presence of Jesus, decide to live like him, empowered by his Spirit. You don't have to live perfectly. You don't have to be anything other than who you are. God in his power and grace has created you for a specific purpose to reveal a specific aspect of his heart to the world. Simply choose to let him in to all you are and do today that your day might be filled with his life-giving presence. Choose to carry his wisdom, love, and grace into relationship with others that in your communication, emotions, and actions you would proclaim his character.

Take time in guided prayer to find rest and purpose in the presence of Christ.

105

GUIDED PRAYER

1. Meditate on God's command to abide in him. Allow Scripture to fill you with desire to center your life around the presence of God.

"Whoever confesses that Jesus is the Son of God, God abides in him, and he in God. So we have come to know and to believe the love that God has for us. God is love, and whoever abides in love abides in God, and God abides in him. By this is love perfected with us, so that we may have confidence for the day of judgment, because as he is so also are we in this world." 1 John 4:15-17

2. Ask God for a revelation of his nearness. Take time to rest in his presence that you might be empowered by the Holy Spirit.

"Be still, and know that I am God. I will be exalted among the nations, I will be exalted in the earth!" Psalm 46:10

"But you will receive power when the Holy Spirit has come upon you, and you will be my witnesses in Jerusalem and in all Judea and Samaria, and to the end of the earth." Acts 1:8

3. Ask God for specific ways in which you can love others today. Pay attention as he puts people or circumstances on your heart. Pay attention to how he would have you engage others today. Ask him for his grace and power to love others well today.

"For we are his workmanship, created in Christ Jesus for good works, which God prepared beforehand, that we should walk in them." Ephesians 2:10

In 1 John 2:6 John writes, *"Whoever says he abides in him ought to walk in the same way in which he walked."* What good are words or desires if we don't put action to them? What does all our talk mean if we never do something about it? The kingdom of God is one that doesn't separate faith and works. James writes, *"Show me your faith apart from your works, and I will show you my faith by my works"* (James 2:18). Choose today to put action to what's in your heart. Don't hold back your love for others. Don't refrain from encouraging and loving other people, even if it's abnormal behavior for you. Step into situations and bring the presence and will of Christ. May your day be marked by the powerful anointing of the Holy Spirit to love others as Jesus did.

Extended Reading: 1 John 4

The wonder of Christmas

WEEK

"And the Word became flesh and dwelt among us, and we have seen his glory, glory as of the only Son from the Father, full of grace and truth." John 1:14

Christmas is a time where we as believers celebrate God's heart to write himself into our story. Prior to Jesus we had no real picture of God's love. All we had to know him by was through stories of old and commandments written into law. But only in Jesus was a pathway created whereby we could walk in intimacy with the Father again. Only in Jesus was the veil torn allowing God's manifest presence into the earth. We owe all that we have to Jesus. We owe all that we have to Christmas. May these four days be filled with joyful worship as we celebrate our newborn King.

Incarnation

DAY 22

DEVOTIONAL

The more of my being I intentionally give to God, the more of my time, energy, and devotion I invest into an abiding connection, the more I begin to sense at my core the power of God's incarnation.

Throughout human history civilizations have looked for God. They've looked for God in the stars. They've looked for God in the elements. They've looked for God in themselves.

A great mystery of Christianity, a mystery that holds real power for our lives, is that while so many look for God and fail to find him, there is nowhere we can go that he is not there.

In Acts 17:28 Paul tells us that it is in Christ that we *"live and move and have our being."* Psalm 139:7-10 says, *"Where shall I go from your Spirit? Or where shall I flee from your presence? If I ascend to heaven, you are there! If I make my bed in Sheol, you are there! If I take the wings of the morning and dwell in the uttermost parts of the sea, even there your hand shall lead me, and your right hand shall hold me."*

And most visibly at Christmas, we celebrate the incarnation of God in the person of Jesus:

"And the Word became flesh and dwelt among us, and we have seen his glory, glory as of the only Son from the Father, full of grace and truth." John 1:14

*"And the Word became flesh and dwelt among us,
and we have seen his glory, glory as of the only Son
from the Father, full of grace and truth."*

JOHN 1:14

But maybe the greatest opportunity in the first coming of Christ is not that he took on flesh for a 33 year period, but that God has always dwelled with us. From the first garden in Genesis to the great city in Revelation, God has never wished to be distant from us. His plan was never to veil himself.

He is always working, always speaking, always revealing, always incarnating himself among us.

The definition of incarnation is a person who embodies in the flesh a deity, spirit, or abstract quality. 1 Corinthians 6:19 tells us that we are now the temple of the Spirit. In Matthew 25:40 Jesus says that our acts of love are ultimately done unto him saying, *"Truly, I say to you, as you did it to one of the least of these my brothers, you did it to me."*

In setting our eyes on the incarnation of God in Jesus, may our eyes be opened to see the incarnation of Christ still among us. And as we seek and find the reality of God in and around us, may that reality deepen our abiding connection to this God who loves us so deeply that he would so wholly dwell among us.

As we pray, may God open the eyes of our hearts to reveal the riches of our inheritance in Christ incarnate (Eph. 1:18).

GUIDED PRAYER

1. As we begin, reflect on the incarnation of God in the person of Jesus. Think about the sacrifice Jesus made to take on flesh and dwell among us. Think about the depth of God's love that he would accept the limitations of humanity for our sake, how deeply he desires to know and be known by us.

"And the Word became flesh and dwelt among us, and we have seen his glory, glory as of the only Son from the Father, full of grace and truth." John 1:14

2. Next reflect on the reality that God dwells in you. In a way, you are called to be an incarnation of God, expressing his loving nature in your uniqueness. Take time to focus on the connection between your spirit and the Spirit of God.

"Do you not know that your body is a temple of the Holy Spirit within you, whom you have from God? You are not your own" 1 Corinthians 6:19

3. How can you, in your uniqueness, incarnate the love of God today? How in this Christmas season do those around you need to see Christ in you? Ask God for insight, and commit to embodying more fully the Spirit of God in you.

"Beloved, let us love one another, for love is from God, and whoever loves has been born of God and knows God." 1 John 4:7

As you go about your day today, looking forward to Christmas, begin to frame your values around finding and keeping a real connection to God's presence with you. Seek to pay attention to ways he might be speaking to you, or leading you, that come from that place of relationship with God. Seek to see God in others around you, knowing that everyone represents the imago dei, a being made in the image of God. And allow yourself to sense the saturation of God's presence that comes when we see him not as vastly separate but truly filling and moving around us.

Extended Reading: John 1

Interdependence

DAY 23

DEVOTIONAL

Yesterday we explored the incarnation of Christ, that in ways beyond the coming of Jesus God has and continues to fill and dwell among us.

Today I want to explore a facet of Christ's incarnation—what it means for us to be interdependent with God and each other. And how in interdependence, in seeing ourselves more through the lens of relationship, we find true abundant life.

In our western world, we see ourselves and others through the lens of individualism. We pride ourselves on self-sufficiency, and expect others to do the same. We systematize the value of personal success, valuing freedom for individual gain at times over the well-being of the world around us.

But if we remove the lens of our western perspective before looking at Scripture, if we free ourselves from our value system of individualism before coming to God, I think we'll find his way to be quite different from ours.

There is no image of God that does not factor in free and paradoxical relationship. God himself is three and one. Father, Son, and Spirit in perfect relationship comprise the idea of God, a concept we cannot grasp on this side of heaven. You and I are both the imago dei, the image of God ourselves, but also as part of God's body in which he is the head. Jesus tells us that he is the vine, and we are the branches. It is in relationship alone that we bear fruit.

> *"That there may be no division in the body, but that the members may have the same care for one another. If one member suffers, all suffer together; if one member is honored, all rejoice together."*
>
> **1 CORINTHIANS 12:25-26**

While God has made us all unique, and expresses himself in our uniqueness, he has not made us self-sufficient.

In God's incarnation at Christmas, we see most visibly the lengths God is willing to go to show that he dwells among us. But it is not in the person of Jesus alone that God has made himself available. In fact, it's through the sacrifice of Jesus on the cross that God has redeemed what was lost, and now in fact dwells in you and in me.

So my encouragement for you today as we near Christmas is this: this Christmas take off the lens of your individualism, even for a few days, and begin to see yourself as a part of a whole.

See yourself as a branch connected to the vine of God. That apart from him we wither. Connected to him we bear fruit. Not just in your time alone with him, but throughout your day, seek to maintain a depth of connection in all you do. Do no work apart from an awareness of him. See others through his eyes. Recognize that it is in God that we *"live and move and have our being"* (Acts 17:38). And enjoy a different way of living, the way of a triune God that invites us into his perfect relationship.

Today in prayer practice your interdependence. Lay down your notions of individualism. Pick up your identity as a part of a whole. Sense the connection between your spirit and the Spirit of God. And seek to live today as a beautiful and unique part of the family and work of God in, through, and around you.

GUIDED PRAYER

1. As we begin, take some time to lay down your individualism. Surrender your pride. Surrender a value for self-sufficiency. And rest in the freedom of needing and wanting God.

"Blessed are the poor in spirit, for theirs is the kingdom of heaven." Matthew 5:3

2. Next, reflect on the notion of being a branch attached to the vine of God. Think about the times you've tried to produce fruit on your own. Then think about the ease and peace of producing fruit as a natural byproduct of abiding in God. Rest in the freedom from needing to accomplish, to produce, to support all on your own.

"I am the vine; you are the branches. Whoever abides in me and I in him, he it is that bears much fruit, for apart from me you can do nothing." John 15:5

3. Last, meditate on the reality of being a part of the whole. Allow your focus to expand to think about those you love, your church, your neighborhood. Think about believers and people stretched around the world. Allow God to give you his heart for his people, and to help you gain a sense of loving connection and interdependence.

"That there may be no division in the body, but that the members may have the same care for one another. If one member suffers, all suffer together; if one member is honored, all rejoice together." 1 Corinthians 12:25-26

In *No Man is an Island* Thomas Merton writes, "The beginning of love is the will to let those we love be perfectly themselves, the resolution not to twist them to fit our own image. If in loving them we do not love what they are, but only their potential likeness to ourselves, then we do not love them: we only love the reflection of ourselves we find in them."

As we move into Christmas Eve tomorrow, take time today to allow the notion of interdependence to prepare you to love those you might spend time with just as they are. While retaining a healthy notion of boundaries, seek to develop a true empathy and awareness of the state of those around you. Try to simply notice while reserving judgement, and develop the capacity to love them in whatever way you feel they need most.

Extended Reading: 1 Corinthians 12

The Sacrifice of Christmas

DAY 24

DEVOTIONAL

On this wonderful Christmas Eve let's take a moment to reflect on the heart of Jesus. Let's take a moment to meditate on the depth of his love for us. It must have been love and love alone that would cause God to take on flesh and dwell among us. It must have been love alone that would give him the desire to leave perfection and take on the suffering and limitations of a human being. Think of the differences! Think of the implications of his decision! Can you

> *"I am the living bread that came down from heaven. If anyone eats of this bread, he will live forever. And the bread that I will give for the life of the world is my flesh."*
>
> **JOHN 6:51**

imagine being the Maker of heaven and earth and choosing to make yourself low unto the point of death for the sake of humans who have gone astray?

For us Christmas is a time of great rejoicing. It's a time of joy, nostalgia, and fond remembrance. For Jesus, it was a time of great sacrifice.

Jesus says in John 6:51, *"I am the living bread that came down from heaven. If anyone eats of this bread, he will live forever. And the bread that I will give for the life of the world is my flesh."* You and I have been afforded eternal life in utter perfection because of the magnitude of Jesus' love for us. We've been granted boundless communion with our Creator simply because he made a way for us where we couldn't. Isaiah 53:4-6 says,

Surely he has borne our griefs and carried our sorrows; yet we esteemed him stricken, smitten by God, and afflicted. But he was pierced for our transgressions; he was crushed for our iniquities; upon him was the chastisement that brought us peace, and with his wounds we are healed. All we like sheep have gone astray; we have turned—every one—to his own way; and the Lord has laid on him the iniquity of us all.

As we celebrate this Christmas Eve, let's remember what Jesus carried in his heart for us prior to his birth. Let's remember the depth of his love for us that he would subject himself to flesh. Let's press into communion with God and give God the only gift he's after: our hearts. And let's worship our Bread of Life in whom we've been granted the eternal gift of relationship with our heavenly Father.

GUIDED PRAYER

1. Meditate on John 6:51. Reflect on the life you've been given because Jesus chose to be born for you.

"I am the living bread that came down from heaven. If anyone eats of this bread, he will live forever. And the bread that I will give for the life of the world is my flesh." John 6:51

2. Take time to meditate on the depth of love Jesus has for you. Allow a revelation of his love to sink past your mind and into your heart that you might find purpose and joy in God's presence.

"Surely he has borne our griefs and carried our sorrows; yet we esteemed him stricken, smitten by God, and afflicted. But he was pierced for our transgressions; he was crushed for our iniquities; upon him was the chastisement that brought us peace, and with his wounds we are healed. All we like sheep have gone astray; we have turned—every one—to his own way; and the Lord has laid on him the iniquity of us all." Isaiah 53:4-6

3. Worship Jesus in response to his great love. Allow his sacrifice to stir up your heart to give him what he was after all along: relationship with you.

"Glory to God in the highest, and on earth peace among those with whom he is pleased!" Luke 2:14

Christmas is a unique opportunity where so much of the world stops and in some way acknowledges the celebration of Jesus' birth. It's a time where hearts are softer to receiving the reality of God's love. Look for opportunities today with your family and friends to join in God's pursuit of their hearts. Look for opportunities to proclaim the availability of life-giving relationship with God. Love them well. Speak life and grace over them. And discover the profound joy God has over those he is drawing to himself, including you. May this Christmas Eve be filled with laughter and celebration given to you as good gifts from the heart of God.

Extended Reading: John 6

Overflowing Joy

DEVOTIONAL

In Luke 2:8-14, the Bible describes a beautiful event around the time of Jesus' birth. Scripture says,

And in the same region there were shepherds out in the field, keeping watch over their flock by night. And an angel of the Lord appeared to them, and the glory of the Lord shone around them, and they were filled with great fear.

*"Though you have not seen him, you love him. Though
you do not now see him, you believe in him and rejoice
with joy that is inexpressible and filled with glory."*

1 PETER 1:8

*And the angel said to them, "Fear not, for behold, I bring
you good news of great joy that will be for all the people.
For unto you is born this day in the city of David a
Savior, who is Christ the Lord. And this will be a sign
for you: you will find a baby wrapped in swaddling cloths
and lying in a manger." And suddenly there was with
the angel a multitude of the heavenly host praising God
and saying, "Glory to God in the highest, and on earth
peace among those with whom he is pleased!"*

This passage contains my favorite phrase in the Christmas story: *"good news of great joy that will be for all the people."* The birth of Jesus was intended to be a celebration of great joy for everyone. With all of humanity in his heart, God sent his only son. With an overwhelming desire to have restored relationship with his people, God came down in the flesh that we might learn of the good news of his unconditional love.

God's intention for you and me is to be a people of great joy. We've been given the greatest gift the world has ever known in Jesus. New life, eternal redemption, and unhindered relationship with our Creator are ours because of Christmas.

But in order for you and me to receive the overflowing joy available to us in God, we have to choose to center ourselves around who Jesus is. We have to choose to center our emotions, actions, words, thoughts, and decisions around God's unceasing mercy and steadfast love. The world tries to pull our hearts in every direction. Stress, earthly pursuits, and constant pressure mark the hearts and minds of so many. But the miracle of Christmas is that we can set our eyes on God himself. We can see and know who God truly is and gain perspective on even the hardest of circumstances.

Overflowing joy is yours today in the Holy Spirit. Real, abundant life is available to you this Christmas. Just as Jesus died for you, he was born for you. Just as he gave his life on the cross, he gave his throne in heaven to take on flesh. Everything you truly need has been provided for you in the heart of God. May your day be filled with overflowing joy and ceaseless praise as you set your eyes on Jesus, the author of *"good news and great joy that will be for all the people."*

127

GUIDED PRAYER

1. Meditate on Jesus' heart to fill you with overflowing joy. Set your eyes on him and look at his face of love.

"The Lord bless you and keep you; the Lord make his face to shine upon you and be gracious to you; the Lord lift up his countenance upon you and give you peace." Numbers 6:24-26

2. Where do you need joy today? Where do you need peace that transcends circumstances?
"For his anger is but for a moment, and his favor is for a lifetime. Weeping may tarry for the night, but joy comes with the morning." Psalm 30:5

"Now may the Lord of peace himself give you peace at all times in every way. The Lord be with you all." 2 Thessalonians 3:16

3. Open your heart to God and receive what he longs to give. Rest in his unfailing love and boundless joy.

"You make known to me the path of life; in your presence there is fullness of joy; at your right hand are pleasures forevermore." Psalm 16:11

"Though you have not seen him, you love him. Though you do not now see him, you believe in him and rejoice with joy that is inexpressible and filled with glory." 1 Peter 1:8

May you find joy in every little gift God's given you today. Whether it's in opening presents, spending time with family, eating good food, or simply enjoying his presence, God has good and pleasing gifts for you today and every day. May his love for you be a foundation on which you can fully enjoy everything in your life. May his grace sustain you through any circumstance. May his face shine upon you that your heart might be filled with peace.

Extended Reading: Luke 2

Looking forward

05

WEEK

"For I know the plans I have for you,
declares the Lord, plans for welfare
and not for evil, to give you a future
and a hope." Jeremiah 29:11

WEEKLY OVERVIEW

As this year comes to a close, it's vital that we take time to both reflect on what God has done and allow him to prepare us for what's to come. A new year marks a fresh opportunity to center our lives around the goodness of God. I pray that as you begin looking toward what is to come you will make space to gain God's perspective, ground your hopes and pursuits on his grace, and celebrate all that God has done and is doing. May your time with God this week be filled with the loving presence of your heavenly Father.

Seasons with God

DEVOTIONAL

The seasons of the year created by the powerful hands of our heavenly Father speak of the need to slow down, stop, and reflect. Times of reflection create space for God's Spirit to speak, helping us remember what he has done, making us aware of what he is doing, and stirring our hearts for what he wants to do next. God loves to use a change in season to remind us to center our lives around his pervasive works.

"For everything there is a season, and a
time for every matter under heaven."

ECCLESIASTES 3:1

Whether it be a change in jobs, weather, moving, or the approaching of a new year, it's crucial that we make space for God to speak to us and prepare us for the wonderful things he has planned.

Ecclesiastes 3:1-5 illustrates this principle in saying,

For everything there is a season, and a time for every matter under heaven: a time to be born, and a time to die; a time to plant, and a time to pluck up what is planted; a time to kill, and a time to heal; a time to break down, and a time to build up; a time to weep, and a time to laugh; a time to mourn, and a time to dance; a time to cast away stones, and a time to gather stones together; a time to embrace, and a time to refrain from embracing.

The best place to begin reflection is in remembering. I don't know whether this year was one filled with heartache or laughter for you. I don't know whether you experienced loss or new beginnings. I don't know whether you cried tears of joy or sadness. But your heavenly Father does. And it's in quiet remembrance that he wants to comfort you, rejoice with you, and wrap you in his arms. It's in remembrance that he wants to bring about healing, grace, love, and perspective. Take time today to remember.

Next, take time to ask the Holy Spirit for revelation on the present. Just as seasons help us to remember the past, they beg of us to live in the present. God is doing a mighty work in and around you right now. This is a time for faith and deep encounters with the transforming love of God. This is a time to savor the beauty of the current and to rest in the goodness of the immediate. God is present to meet with you, love you, and fill you. He has strength, grace, comfort, and joy for you if you will make space to receive the fullness of what he wants to give. Take time today to savor.

Lastly, God longs to fill you with hope and expectancy for his future plans. The new year, filled with its possibilities and new beginnings, is quickly approaching. Your heavenly Father, who dwells in all of eternity, longs to prepare you for what is to come. He longs to lay a foundation for your year with a fresh revelation of his love, faithfulness, and presence. He longs to fill you with hope and desires that he will see through to fruition. Take time today to allow him to prepare you for all next year holds.

May your time in guided prayer be marked by clarity and revelation in the Holy Spirit as you engage in these three practices.

GUIDED PRAYER

1. Reflect on this past year. What were your triumphs? What were your failures? How did God meet you in both? Allow him to comfort you in any pain and rejoice with you in any victory.

"Know therefore that the Lord your God is God, the faithful God who keeps covenant and steadfast love with those who love him and keep his commandments, to a thousand generations." Deuteronomy 7:9

"Blessed be the God and Father of our Lord Jesus Christ, the Father of mercies and God of all comfort, who comforts us in all our affliction, so that we may be able to comfort those who are in any affliction, with the comfort with which we ourselves are comforted by God." 2 Corinthians 1:3-4

"The Lord your God is in your midst, a mighty one who will save; he will rejoice over you with gladness; he will quiet you by his love; he will exult over you with loud singing." Zephaniah 3:17

2. What is God doing right now? What is he teaching and instilling in you? What is he calling you to savor?

"Therefore do not be anxious, saying, 'What shall we eat?' or 'What shall we drink?' or 'What shall we wear?' For the Gentiles seek after all these things, and your heavenly Father knows that you need them all. But seek first the kingdom of God and his righteousness, and all these things will be added to you. Therefore do not be anxious about tomorrow, for tomorrow will be anxious for itself. Sufficient for the day is its own trouble." Matthew 6:31-34

3. Ask God to plant hopes and dreams for next year in your heart. What do you want to see happen personally next year? What do you hope God does in and through you? What works has he prepared for you?

"Trust in the Lord with all your heart, and do not lean on your own understanding. In all your ways acknowledge him, and he will make straight your paths." Proverbs 3:5-6

"For we are his workmanship, created in Christ Jesus for good works, which God prepared beforehand, that we should walk in them." Ephesians 2:10

"For I know the plans I have for you, declares the Lord, plans for welfare and not for evil, to give you a future and a hope." Jeremiah 29:11

May Galatians 6:7-10 stir within you a commitment to fully engage in the season in which God has you:

Do not be deceived: God is not mocked, for whatever one sows, that will he also reap. For the one who sows to his own flesh will from the flesh reap corruption, but the one who sows to the Spirit will from the Spirit reap eternal life. And let us not grow weary of doing good, for in due season we will reap, if we do not give up. So then, as we have opportunity, let us do good to everyone, and especially to those who are of the household of faith.

Extended Reading: Psalm 1

New Beginnings

DAY 27

DEVOTIONAL

A new year marks a new beginning: a time for the children of God to reground themselves in the love of the Father. God loves to use new seasons to remind us of his desire to continually make us new. From winter to spring we see that which appeared dead burst forth into beautiful arrays of God's glorious work. And God longs for the same fresh start in our lives as he does for his creation. He longs to make things new as the new year begins.

"The steadfast love of the Lord never ceases; his mercies never come to an end; they are new every morning; great is your faithfulness. 'The Lord is my portion,' says my soul, 'therefore I will hope in him.'"

LAMENTATIONS 3:22-24

Lamentations 3:22-24 says, *"The steadfast love of the Lord never ceases; his mercies never come to an end; they are new every morning; great is your faithfulness. 'The Lord is my portion,' says my soul, 'therefore I will hope in him.'"* We have hope in the steadfast love of God. His powerful love can make new all that needs restoration. God's heart is to free you from that which weighs you down and robs you of the abundant life Jesus came to bring you.

With this year coming to a close and a new year fast approaching, it's time for us to gain perspective on that which needs rebirth. Whatever sin has entangled you this year does not have to gain victory over you in the next. Whatever lie you've believed that's wrecked your emotions, thoughts, and actions does not have to win the battle over your mind next year. Whatever wound or disappointment that has hurt you can be healed and reborn to empower you for that which is to come.

God's heart is to meet you where you are today. He longs to meet you at your greatest point of weakness and pain and wrap you up in his love. He longs for you to know he is with you, for you, and will walk with you into newness of life. *"His mercies never come to an end; they are new every morning"* (Lamentations 3:22-23). God has limitless, powerful grace for you today. Run to him with your sin. Run to him with your failures and struggles. Run to him with the pain of others' words that he might speak his healing truth over you.

Your heavenly Father loves you and is for you. He has new beginnings in store for you. But just as a tree needs fresh sunlight, warmth, and rain to bear fruit again, you need the refreshing rain of God's grace and the warmth of his steadfast love to be made new. You can't do it on your own. You weren't made to do it on your own. All you need for a new beginning is wholly available in the arms of your loving Father. Open up your heart to him today and receive the newness of life he paid the highest price to give.

141

GUIDED PRAYER

1. Meditate on God's desire and ability to lead you to a new beginning. Reflect on his power over sin, his heart to comfort, and his ability to shepherd.

"For our sake he made him to be sin who knew no sin, so that in him we might become the righteousness of God." 2 Corinthians 5:21

"He heals the brokenhearted and binds up their wounds." Psalm 147:3

"For the Lamb in the midst of the throne will be their shepherd, and he will guide them to springs of living water, and God will wipe away every tear from their eyes." Revelation 7:17

2. Where do you need a new beginning? What sin do you need freedom from? What wound do you need healed? Where do you need new life?

3. Run to God with your sin, pain, failures, and frustrations and open your heart to receive his powerful presence. Ask him to show you the path to victory over sin. Ask him to reveal his plan for healing your wounds. Rest in his loving arms today and allow his presence to be enough.

"I have said these things to you, that in me you may have peace. In the world you will have tribulation. But take heart; I have overcome the world." John 16:33

"Blessed is the man who remains steadfast under trial, for when he has stood the test he will receive the crown of life, which God has promised to those who love him." James 1:12

"My presence will go with you, and I will give you rest." Exodus 33:14

Oftentimes the road to a new beginning is wrought with a host of mistakes and defeats. But know that to continue on the path side by side with the Holy Spirit is a victory in itself. Don't give up on new life. Seek the fullness of God's goodness with all your might. Allow him to help you, forgive you, and strengthen you along the way. He will be faithful to shepherd you into all his wonderful plans. All you have to do is follow his leadership and enjoy his nearness. May you find comfort and hope in the powerful presence of your loving Father today.

Extended Reading: Psalm 23

143

You Can Do All Things

DAY 28

DEVOTIONAL

"I can do all things through him who strengthens me" (Philippians 4:13). Do you know that your God longs to strengthen you? This verse illustrates a powerful spiritual principle that our heavenly Father longs for you to know today. You were never meant to go through this life alone, living in your own strength. The God who formed the mountains, filled the seas, breathed life into dust, and sustains every living creature longs to strengthen you for whatever lies ahead.

*"I can do all things through
him who strengthens me."*

PHILIPPIANS 4:13

Ephesians 3:20-21 says, *"Now to him who is able to do far more abundantly than all that we ask or think, according to the power at work within us, to him be glory in the church and in Christ Jesus throughout all generations, forever and ever. Amen."* God can do *"far more abundantly"* than you could ever dream in your life, *"according to the power at work within [you]."* The Holy Spirit, the power of God for all the earth, dwells within you. Just as he empowered the Apostles for the advance of the gospel through trial and tribulation, he will empower you. Just as he spoke to the Apostles, telling them where they should go and what they should do, he longs to lead you.

You can do all that God has called you to. Whether it be victory over sin, engaging in difficult confession, working biblically rather than according to the world, seeking unity and fellowship with those that bother you, or simply seeking God with all your heart, the Holy Spirit will strengthen you today if you are willing to receive.

To be strengthened by God begins by declaring our inability. God says, *"My grace is sufficient for you, for my power is made perfect in weakness"* (2 Corinthians 12:9). When we try and live in our own strength, we become unable to receive the grace of God. God's grace is never forced on us, but rather it is readily available to all those who acknowledge their need of it. God cannot empower you to experience unity with a fellow believer if you try and engage in relationship apart from the inner work of the Holy Spirit. He cannot empower you to experience victory from sin if you don't take time to receive his love and follow his leadership moment by moment.

To be strengthened by the mighty hand of God is to stop living in your own strength and instead wholly rely on his. God longs to *"do far more abundantly than all [you] ask or think"* if you will lean into him for his love, power, and guidance. He has plans far above anything you could ever dream of, and the path to those plans begins with following him moment by moment today. He will faithfully guide you into all the abundant life he has for you, but you must be willing to follow him and live by his strength.

Take time in guided prayer to meditate on the strength of God available to you, acknowledge your need of his help, and receive his grace.

145

GUIDED PRAYER

1. Meditate on God's desire to empower you to do all he has planned for you.

"I can do all things through him who strengthens me." Philippians 4:13

"I have been crucified with Christ. It is no longer I who live, but Christ who lives in me. And the life I now live in the flesh I live by faith in the Son of God, who loved me and gave himself for me." Galatians 2:20

"I know how to be brought low, and I know how to abound. In any and every circumstance, I have learned the secret of facing plenty and hunger, abundance and need. I can do all things through him who strengthens me." Philippians 4:12-13

2. Acknowledge your need of God's help in every area. Tell him you need his help for victory over sin, your relationships, and for the tasks set before you.

"For sin will have no dominion over you, since you are not under law but under grace." Romans 6:14

"I therefore, a prisoner for the Lord, urge you to walk in a manner worthy of the calling to which you have been called, with all humility and gentleness, with patience, bearing with one another in love, eager to maintain the unity of the Spirit in the bond of peace." Ephesians 4:1-3

"Now to him who is able to do far more abundantly than all that we ask or think, according to the power at work within us, to him be glory in the church and in Christ Jesus throughout all generations, forever and ever. Amen." Ephesians 3:20-21

3. Take time to receive God's presence and experience his grace. Ask him to fill you with a desire for holiness. Ask him to fill you with love for others. Ask him to reveal his path to you today that you might follow his leading moment by moment.

"As obedient children, do not be conformed to the passions of your former ignorance, but as he who called you is holy, you also be holy in all your conduct, since it is written, 'You shall be holy, for I am holy.'" 1 Peter 1:14-16

"A new commandment I give to you, that you love one another: just as I have loved you, you also are to love one another." John 13:34

"Where shall I go from your Spirit? Or where shall I flee from your presence? If I ascend to heaven, you are there! If I make my bed in Sheol, you are there! If I take the wings of the morning and dwell in the uttermost parts of the sea, even there your hand shall lead me, and your right hand shall hold me." Psalm 139:7-10

In the context of our verse for today, Paul describes an important spiritual principle in Philippians 4:11-13:

Not that I am speaking of being in need, for I have learned in whatever situation I am to be content. I know how to be brought low, and I know how to abound. In any and every circumstance, I have learned the secret of facing plenty and hunger, abundance and need. I can do all things through him who strengthens me.

Trust God in whatever season he's leading you through. Whether you find yourself with plenty or little, difficulties or ease, you can find your contentment in the gift of abundant relationship with your heavenly Father. All that is good comes from his hands alone. May you be strengthened to find joy, peace, and contentment in the presence of your loving Father.

Extended Reading: Philippians 4

Hope in God's Nearness

DAY 29

DEVOTIONAL

As sons and daughters of the living God, faith founded on God's nearness should be at the core of our hope for next year. Psalm 139:7-12 says,

Where shall I go from your Spirit? Or where shall I flee from your presence? If I ascend to heaven, you are there! If I make my bed in Sheol, you are there! If I take the

*"Let your steadfast love, O Lord, be
upon us, even as we hope in you."*

PSALM 33:22

wings of the morning and dwell in the uttermost parts of the sea, even there your hand shall lead me, and your right hand shall hold me. If I say, "Surely the darkness shall cover me, and the light about me be night," even the darkness is not dark to you; the night is bright as the day, for darkness is as light with you.

There is no greater source of hope than God's resounding declaration of his nearness. Jesus paid the ultimate price that you and I might be no longer separated from God. His presence now dwells within us through the Holy Spirit. And that fact brings a pervasive hope that has the ability to profoundly impact every aspect of our lives.

As you look forward, know that the God who dwells within you knows every little thing that will happen next year. He dwells within all of eternity. Time for him is not as it is for us. And he promises to be with you in the midst of any trial, pain, victory, or defeat. He longs for you to know his presence moment by moment in everything you will do.

Your heavenly Father says, *"Fear not, for I am with you; be not dismayed, for I am your God; I will strengthen you, I will help you, I will uphold you with my righteous right hand"* (Isaiah 41:10). You can have the fullness of hope for next year because the God who fashioned time is *"your God."* He will help you and be there for you. He will never *"leave you or forsake you"* (Deuteronomy 31:6).

While the rest of the world sits in fear and worry over what the future holds, your God is leading you in the path of peace that comes from trusting in his presence. But the choice is yours. Will you place your hope in yourself, others, the world, or in God? If you try and build your hope on the foundations of this world, you will find yourself tossed about by the ever-changing waves of man's opinion. But if you choose to found your hope on the rock of God's nearness, your life will be filled with all the goodness and mercy of God's steadfast love.

Take time right now to place your hope in the loving nearness of your heavenly Father as you enter into guided prayer.

GUIDED PRAYER

1. Allow Scripture to fill you with hope founded on the nearness of God.

"Where shall I go from your Spirit? Or where shall I flee from your presence? If I ascend to heaven, you are there! If I make my bed in Sheol, you are there! If I take the wings of the morning and dwell in the uttermost parts of the sea, even there your hand shall lead me, and your right hand shall hold me. If I say, "Surely the darkness shall cover me, and the light about me be night," even the darkness is not dark to you; the night is bright as the day, for darkness is as light with you." Psalm 139:7-12

"And he said, 'My presence will go with you, and I will give you rest.'" Exodus 33:14

"Be strong and courageous. Do not fear or be in dread of them, for it is the Lord your God who goes with you. He will not leave you or forsake you." Deuteronomy 31:6

2. Where do you need the peace and comfort that comes from knowing God is and will always be near to you? What are you worried about for next year? What unknowns are causing you stress or fear?

3. Take time to place your hope in the nearness of your heavenly Father. Place your trust in him that he will always be with you through thick and thin.

"Fear not, for I am with you; be not dismayed, for I am your God; I will strengthen you, I will help you, I will uphold you with my righteous right hand." Isaiah 41:10

Why do we live as if God isn't near to us? Why do we fumble through life on our own when Jesus paid the ultimate price that we might have restored relationship with our loving Creator? God has made available a better way of living and has called us to walk in it. He wants us to know his will, love, and power moment by moment. He wants our thoughts, emotions, and actions to be fully founded in his unshakable nearness. Paul's prayer in Romans 15:13 is my prayer for you today: *"May the God of hope fill you with all joy and peace in believing, so that by the power of the Holy Spirit you may abound in hope."* May your day be filled with the peace that comes from trusting in God's nearness.

Extended Reading: Psalm 139

Dream

DEVOTIONAL

God longs for his children to dream. He longs for us to set aside time with him to wish and wonder about what life could be. I fear that many Christians have lost the art of dreaming with God out of a misunderstanding of his heart. While God most definitely has a will for our lives, he also longs for us to dream with him so that his desires become our own. While he most definitely has perfect plans for us, he longs for us to want his plans that we might co-labor with him rather than being dragged by him like an ill-tempered child into what's

*"Delight yourself in the Lord, and he will
give you the desires of your heart."*

PSALM 37:4

best. May we make time today as the new year approaches to dream with God that our hearts may be filled with his longings and desires.

The chief way in which God wants to lead you is by planting dreams in your heart and then satisfying those dreams. Psalm 37:4 says, *"Delight yourself in the Lord, and he will give you the desires of your heart."* Our Father longs for us to be so delighted in him that we would want what he wants. He longs to fill us with right desires and then satisfy those desires in his perfect timing and in his perfect way. He longs for us to trust him as our good Shepherd to such a depth that we joyfully follow him wherever he leads.

You see, Psalm 37:4 is more about delighting ourselves in God than getting what we currently think we want most. It's more about the pursuit of him as our chief joy than anything we could receive from him. God alone knows what's best for us. He alone has the perspective and wisdom to shepherd us to a truly abundant life. And we will never follow someone we don't trust has our best will at heart.

To make God our chief joy is to surrender our lives to the overwhelming goodness and grace of an omnipotent, omnipresent, and fully loving Father. God is both willing and able to lead us into the fullness of abundant life. He is both willing and able to fill us with right longings and desires if we will simply open our hearts and trust him.

Until we center our hearts, and therefore our lives, totally and completely around the goodness and will of our heavenly Father, we will never experience all this life has to offer. The gateway to living filled and satisfied is simply enjoying God and allowing our hearts to become like his.

Know today that your heavenly Father longs to dream with you. He longs to hear what it is you most desire. He longs to have conversation with you about what's best. And he longs to be your chief joy, that the greatest cry of your heart is to delight yourself in him and receive whatever comes with fully restored, unbridled relationship with him. May your day be marked by a filling of new desires from your loving Father.

153

GUIDED PRAYER

1. Meditate on God's heart to be your chief joy and to dream with you.

"Delight yourself in the Lord, and he will give you the desires of your heart." Psalm 37:4

"For I know the plans I have for you, declares the Lord, plans for welfare and not for evil, to give you a future and a hope." Jeremiah 29:11

"But seek first the kingdom of God and his righteousness, and all these things will be added to you." Matthew 6:33

2. In what ways do you need to make God your chief joy? What have you placed above him in your heart? What are you looking to for joy, security, and fulfillment above God?

3. Take time to enjoy God and ask him to fill you with dreams and desires. In his presence take note of what you long for. Ask him to transform your heart that you may desire what he wants.

"If you then, who are evil, know how to give good gifts to your children, how much more will your Father who is in heaven give good things to those who ask him!" Matthew 7:11

"For the Lord God is a sun and shield; the Lord bestows favor and honor. No good thing does he withhold from those who walk uprightly." Psalm 84:11

"For our heart is glad in him, because we trust in his holy name." Psalm 33:21

Psalm 37:23-24 says, *"The steps of a man are established by the Lord, when he delights in his way; though he fall, he shall not be cast headlong, for the Lord upholds his hand."* There is no greater pursuit than simply delighting in the Lord. When we delight ourselves in him, life becomes incredibly simple. It's in the mixing of God and the world that our hearts feel burdened and confused. Assess the status of your heart today. To what level are you delighting in God? Will the chief pursuit of your life be God or the world? Get lost in the love of your heavenly Father today and allow your life to become swept up in his overwhelming goodness.

Extended Reading: Psalm 37

Make Space for God to Fill

DAY 31

DEVOTIONAL

The story of Mary, Martha, and Jesus found in Luke 10 encapsulates God's longing for simple, unfettered relationship with his children. As this year comes to a close I pray that this story would set a fire in our hearts to live out of unhindered union with our heavenly Father.

"Be still, and know that I am God. I will be exalted among the nations, I will be exalted in the earth!"

PSALM 46:10

I pray that we would seek to continually make space in our lives for the one thing that truly matters. Scripture says in Luke 10:38-42,

Now as they went on their way, Jesus entered a village. And a woman named Martha welcomed him into her house. And she had a sister called Mary, who sat at the Lord's feet and listened to his teaching. But Martha was distracted with much serving. And she went up to him and said, "Lord, do you not care that my sister has left me to serve alone? Tell her then to help me." But the Lord answered her, "Martha, Martha, you are anxious and troubled about many things, but one thing is necessary. Mary has chosen the good portion, which will not be taken away from her."

I want my life to be centered around *"the good portion."* I want all my days to be marked by choosing to sit at the feet of Jesus rather than living a life based solely on works. At the end of my life, I want to look back and know that I sought relationship with my God above all else, and that I gave him my heart in and out of every season, no matter the cost.

The simple truth of Christian spirituality is that God longs to fill whatever space we make available to him with his nearness. The gift he gives us that far surpasses a spouse, a job, a family, earthly success, or financial stability is simply himself. The heartcry of our heavenly Father is simply this, *"Abide in me, and I in you"* (John 15:4).

What would it look like if your chief New Year's resolution was making space for God to fill? What other desires of your heart would that take care of? How wonderful would it be to experience the transcendent peace and joy that comes from centering your life around meeting with God? How continually satisfied would you feel in consistently receiving the powerful love of your heavenly Father?

Take time today to reflect on what truly matters. Take time to choose *"the good portion"* that your life might be centered around he who alone has the power to truly satisfy your every longing. May your year be marked by unhindered union with the God who fills you with his greatest gift: himself.

157

GUIDED PRAYER

1. Meditate on God being "the good portion." Allow the story of Mary, Martha, and Jesus to fill you with a longing to seek relationship with God above all else.

"Now as they went on their way, Jesus entered a village. And a woman named Martha welcomed him into her house. And she had a sister called Mary, who sat at the Lord's feet and listened to his teaching. But Martha was distracted with much serving. And she went up to him and said, 'Lord, do you not care that my sister has left me to serve alone? Tell her then to help me.' But the Lord answered her, 'Martha, Martha, you are anxious and troubled about many things, but one thing is necessary. Mary has chosen the good portion, which will not be taken away from her.'" Luke 10:38-42

2. Take time to make space for God to fill. Open your heart to him and center your focus on his nearness. Allow Scripture to fill you with faith to receive all he has to offer.

"Seek the Lord and his strength; seek his presence continually!" 1 Chronicles 16:11

"And do not get drunk with wine, for that is debauchery, but be filled with the Spirit." Ephesians 5:18

"You will seek me and find me, when you seek me with all your heart." Jeremiah 29:13

3. Rest in the nearness of God. Cast aside all other concerns, fears, and reservations and simply be with God. He will guide you into all you need, but relationship with him should always be centered around simply sitting at his feet.

"Be still, and know that I am God. I will be exalted among the nations, I will be exalted in the earth!" Psalm 46:10

"And I will ask the Father, and he will give you another Helper, to be with you forever, even the Spirit of truth, whom the world cannot receive, because it neither sees him nor knows him. You know him, for he dwells with you and will be in you." John 14:16-17

"Where shall I go from your Spirit? Or where shall I flee from your presence? If I ascend to heaven, you are there! If I make my bed in Sheol, you are there! If I take the wings of the morning and dwell in the uttermost parts of the sea, even there your hand shall lead me, and your right hand shall hold me." Psalm 139:7-10

If you center your life around abiding in God, your year will be filled with remarkable, heavenly, and eternal impact. May John 15:1-5 fill you with a desire to abide in God that all you do this year may yield lasting fruit:

I am the true vine, and my Father is the vinedresser. Every branch in me that does not bear fruit he takes away, and every branch that does bear fruit he prunes, that it may bear more fruit. Already you are clean because of the word that I have spoken to you. Abide in me, and I in you. As the branch cannot bear fruit by itself, unless it abides in the vine, neither can you, unless you abide in me. I am the vine; you are the branches. Whoever abides in me and I in him, he it is that bears much fruit, for apart from me you can do nothing.

Extended Reading: Luke 10